The Sar Pass Trek

Himalayan Trek With The Touth Hostel Association Of India

Pankaj Ghare

ISBN 978-93-5458-174-8
© Pankaj Ghare 2021
Published in India 2021 by Pencil

A brand of

One Point Six Technologies Pvt. Ltd.
123, Building J2, Shram Seva Premises,
Wadala Truck Terminal, Wadala (E)
Mumbai 400037, Maharashtra, INDIA
E connect@thepencilapp.com
W www.thepencilapp.com

Author biography

Pankaj Ghare is Mechanical Engineer having his own business in Facade Construction. Along with being in the technical field since last 2005; he is also a writer, blogger, and photographer.

He did his schooling at Amar Kor Vidyalaya, Diploma in Mechanical Engineering from Veermata Jijabai Technological Institute (VJTI), Mumbai, and Bachelor of Engineering Sardar Pate College of Engineering (Mumbai).

He published his first book in Marathi named 'Pahile Paul' (First Step based on Sar Pass Trek. This book is an English Edition of the same.
He has also written a book on his cycling experience in Ladakh.

He also writes in his own Marathi Blog.
He has published many articles in various Marathi newspapers and magazines.

He has published 5 E-books in Marathi for the Esahity.com website.

Till now he has successfully done treks more than 100 and some cycling tours in Maharashtra and other states.

CONTENTS

Author biography 3

Epigraph 6

Foreword 8

Acknowledgements 11

Introduction 15

Days after Independence 18

Chalo Delhi 29

Love at First Sight 37

Best Camp - a Base Camp 47

Get-Set-Go 59

A day in a Happy Village 67

Jungle Book 81

Ups, Downs and Ups 91

It's a Victory 107

A Lovely Fear 119

'Rest' is best 128

Good Bye Dear All 133

Night of 24 Hours 143

Restart and Recall 157

Waah Taj !! 168

In search of God 184

First Flight Fun...199

Home Sweet Home 207

Epigraph

Challenges always attract energetic youth and while he is taking a guess as to which challenge he can overcome, he suddenly finds some hint. He persuades it. The challenge transforms into a hobby. Hobby becomes a habit and it boosts him. In this momentum, he accepts the challenge. This puts him at a whole new turn, completely out of the box. At this instant, his eyes are filled with satisfaction in achieving one milestone. This is the "first roar " of one such passionate youth named "Pankaj Ghare" with a vision of " I'm here to do something great". It indeed is an adventure to cultivate the hobby of mountaineering. So he felt intensely that the pinnacle of mountains in the Himalayas is signaling him. And with select fellow mates, he made plans to visit the peaks and even accomplished it. This is a churn of the journey, a migration, not just a story of the journey but it is beyond that. You will get to know this when the story unfolds.

Pankaj has his own writing style. He has vision, simplicity, a good sense of humor, affection towards nature, animals, and above all, he has innocence. Therefore he can do tete-a-tete very easily with his mother (no network signals required!). Pankaj could picture live all funny incidents, infinite hurdles in the journey, cyclic changes in climate, and live like a commando!! I wish you a very Happy Journey!!

 - Prakash Bhatambrekar,
Former Regional Secretary,
Sahity Academy

Foreword

Attraction towards nature challenges some adventurous people. Without thinking about the success or failure the Young generation is facing the natural calamities are climbing over mountains successfully. We can understand the attraction of people towards mountaineering due to the noble behavior of 'Nature' during mountaineering and have a break from commercial routine. But it's unbelievable that an engineer, who is friendly with machines, started wandering in hills, forts; and gets sign by nature, not only turns his feet towards nature with his one call; but he conquers the Himalaya.

Pankaj Ghare is a keen and hard-working student. It was already in his mind at the student stage that he has to do something big. Actually, it was his wish somewhere deep inside. He knows very well about what can him do, what are his capabilities and what is his background and limitation.

It is a great satisfaction that Pankaj Ghare, looking towards a life with the sportsman spirit, not only conquers the Himalaya but also puts his experience into words.

I feel admire while praising his courage. His journey not only starts at his home at Bhandup till the top of the Himalayas, but it makes you visualize close observations. Different perceptive of Human being touches your heart. People in the journey, their behavior, hurtful incidents enrich the real-life experience. Increasing bonding with friends in the journey, recalling pleasant memories of home, school, college; anxiousness to talk with mother at peak of the mountain, calling home for informing about a safe return, not being able to talk with father, are so many incidents which the reader will remember forever.

Accident at a distance of 14 Kim from Sundar Nagar in a next journey depresses. Without stopping there, they start the journey with determination. On a flight journey commenting others about their inexperience (though he himself is new to the flight journey), eagerness to reach home, attachment towards the homemade food; is attractive and readable.

He accepts and thanks sincerely without forgetting the Youth Hostel Association of India for their happiness. Discipline and cleanliness by Youth Hostel teach a lot. The writer says, "Their perspective got enlarged like Himalaya while being with Youth Hostel. We started looking for more heights of dreams. We started planning the next imaginary plans. Andaman- Nikobar or a desert in Rajasthan, north-east of India or Lakshadweep-Kanyakumari?" Shadow of sadness went away while traveling. The indescribable situation at the end of the journey, tears of joy, and peace for a moment, then tears again… and then big jubilation throws away the tiredness of 15 days.

Flowing style, energetic incidents, spattering jokes in this book is making a Ticket available for next-generation and young travelers. Everyone has different experiences and perspectives, approaches towards looking to life. Hence a book bag packed with experience will definitely guide new trekkers. Everyone has a different, thrilling story of accomplishment, and to describe it in words is an attempt beyond the limit. But still, it's admirable. It's honest. Somewhere way of explaining shows self-importance but still, there is innocence. Obviously, it is worth collecting. I congratulate the writer sincerely and wish for his future ahead. I wish readers that this book may inspire them!!

Smt. Meena L. Sawant
M.A., B. Ed.

Acknowledgements

Though I can communicate very well in English my professional life, I could not publish my writing in English unless I could use a dictionary published by Abdus-Salam Chaus. I could understand so many English Words for Marathi words. I am also thankful to Grammarly Extension which helps a lot when writing on a laptop or computer.

I am thankful to Mr. Shreesha Bhat, Mr. Rakes N, (especially) Mr. Amol Sontakkey; both are my co-trekkers, and Mr. Prasad Gaonkar, my college friend who read this book before publishing and gave suggestions and corrections.

Obviously, I have to thank readers of my Marathi Edition from all over the world. That gave me confidence that this book is really good in Marathi but since I have so many friends who were on the same journey I had already decided to publish this when I will get an opportunity.

Now, thank you reader so much for choosing this ticket for reading.

Why I am mentioning it as a Ticket? Because the reader may actually feel that he is traveling. Those who don't like journeys may consider as fiction.

This book was published in Marathi in 2012 and it was my first write up which I could publish on a bigger platform. Since my mother tongue is Marathi I could write and publish in Marathi only. I translated it in 2011-12 when I was not good enough in English. Later I read so many English books to reach the least level of English for publishing this book.

Because of Job and business later I couldn't get time and Lockdown time is used as an opportunity to re-write this edition in English. However, when I read my book, every time feel I am lagging in both the language though it is getting appreciated by every reader till now.

It was my first journey to the Himalayas. Traveling in that direction was also the first time. I traveled in the south zone of India for professional reasons and I could travel there to other nearer locations. But this was the first journey, out of my state Maharashtra, for which I had taken leave.

I could come to know; I could attempt and completed successfully this 'SAR PASS trek' till the 13,800 Feet. This was the main journey in the entire journey and this book. First of all, I am thankful to the Youth Hostel Association of India.

Before conquering this trek, I could do so many treks at Maharashtra in a difficult situation. I could do this because of Mr. Rajesh Parab, Bhandup, and Mr. Vinayak Chavan, Kalyan with whom I did my first trek at Mahuli fort at Maharashtra in the year 2002. I am saying thank you to both of them after 10 years.

I could get introduced to Rock-climbing and other adventure sports in a camp arranged by Newspaper Loksatta. By coincidence, it was the same newspaper where my first article on trekking got published.

Amar Kor Vidyalaya is my school where I did my schooling till SSC. It is beside the mountain only and I consider it as one of the forts. Here I could learn and develop other interests along with my studies. I am indebted to the school.

My teacher, teaching the subject of Marathi language was suggesting everyone write a preface before answers. She writes the Preface for my book. After reading the Preface written by her, I started liking my book. Thank you, Madam.

Distances, height, duration mentioned at a different location in different incidents are real in most of the paragraphs. Somewhere guessing about time, speed, the temperature will be more or less. I could guess and write this because of my diploma course in mechanical engineering at Veermata Jijabai Technological Institute, Mumbai and Bachelor of Engineering at Sardar Patel College of Engineering. I am thankful to both institutes.

Though the main trek was arranged by Youth Hostel, our whole plan, actual plan, changed the plan, its management, and actual participation happened because of special people entered in life. Mr. Amol Sontakkey, Nagpur, Mr. Vishal Suryavanshi, Pune, Mr. Mukesh Mali, Solapur, Mr. Vinayak Chikhale, Mumbai, Mr. Alphin Paul, Mr. Aswant Rajeev, Mr. Rakes N, Mr. Srijeeth, all from Kerala; all were my group members. Their contribution is far away from saying thanks.

I am from an engineering background. I write this book as a simple write-up only for my memories. Mr. Vinay Patil who is a poet guided me about books and introduced me to the literature field and media. I am so thankful to him.

One of the greatest people I met in my life is Mr. Prakash Bhatambrekar actually made me realize the Publication industry.

I met some of the publication houses who rejected me because I and Himalaya both were not 'Big'. Mr. Nitin Hirve from Samvedana Prakashan showed a trust that supports the new writers for their books. He stopped my travel only for publishing. I am thankful for him and an actor Mr. Narayan Jadhav and Prof. Poornima Jaadhav introduced me to him.

Since childhood, my dad brought so many comics which developed my interest and hobby of reading till now. It will be a very very small thing to say only "Thanks" to him.

When I was 1.5 years old, my mother and aunty took me on a small trek at Matond near my village 'Tulas' in Sindhudurga District of Maharashtra. I am not able to say thank you to both of them.

Yours Sincerely,
Pankaj Pratibha-Prakash Ghare

Introduction

Let me have words with you.

Nature is a Natural gift to human beings. You can say it is given to you at your naming ceremony. The sun, Air, Water, Moon, Rain, Birds, Animals, Rivers, Sea, Mountains, Trees, Flowers, Fruits, Colors, Odour…. so many gifts. And there is no tax while enjoying these. While breathing, hearing, having sunbath, while getting shivered, while laughing, crying, and doing so many things you don't need to have permission. You can feel hot in summer and call for rain after getting bored of heat. In a heavy wind, with thunder and lightning rain should shower plenty of water, then we should get bored of mud and say enough for the year, then again have sweat in October then again wait for cool and pleasant weather and again for sunrays. We demand a lot and Nature to make your wish come true. We experience so many things and carry out routine with a cycle of the season. However, at one moment we say, "I could live a better life" or "I have not lived so far".

Because of picnic, tours we could enjoy cold weather in the summer season at Hill Station. Even this we have learned from flying birds. Roaming to get food and then returning to the home, protecting himself and his family is also taught by nature to a human being. Human doesn't have anything like Infinite universe, limitless sky, countless stars, ample of shades of colors, bottomless ocean, high mountains, playful rivers, immature birds, wandering animals. He is neither owner of any of these. I don't understand on what basis Human has made pieces of the earth who born on mother's lap and play over another mother i.e. earth and getting merged somewhere in-universe? That's why Mars and the moon are far away from him!

People say, "Man has invented Wheel". I don't think so. If he could have invented he would shout, "Eureka, Eureka" or "I have done it". He would be publishing his name first then tell about his invention. Do we know the name of that inventor?

Okay. Let's do not criticize. But I appreciate that inventor who has invented the second wheel or the remaining three wheels. Because of him only I could travel a lot!!

Because of the wheel, we could start travel and communicate. Very soon, the earth changed its appearance. Water in a river got stopped; dirty water got mixed in the sea. Sometimes because of acidic rain and because global warming ice started getting melt, water level in the world is started increase. It's a risky time now!

After disturbing a system in Nature Human being is too busy now. Sun has to do duty for 12-12 hours continuously. Moon will be having a monthly leave. Its compulsory duty to work for all other days he will be working as a watchman.

Traveling in vehicles on cement roads, getting pushes everywhere, and hearing so much noise humans started going to the office. Hunger money became important to fulfill the hunger of the body. He started seating in front of a machine named a computer and started behaving like a machine itself. He lowered his years of life but even it became difficult for him to live properly in a time available for him.

But, Nature asked him some time for enjoyment and he is going to nature for picnics and treks; sometimes at Jungle, sometimes at a seashore, at Bank of rivers, under a waterfall to sing. Sometimes he started enjoying twinkling stars at midnight, sometimes even at noon, at heavy rain, or sometimes in cold. He is there to sing the song of life and to live actually.

I want to talk a lot about a similar journey. This write-up is to keep those memories alive permanently dedicated to Chhatrapati Shivaji Maharaj.

– Pankaj Ghare

Days after Independence

1st June 2010, was like Independence Day of my life. I just had completed my 4 years engineering course at Night College in Mumbai. I was working in one of the largest and respected companies in India's private sector. Actually, I didn't have completed my engineering; I had just spent those 4 years. I was eager to do some interesting and memorable in my life & therefore decided to spend maximum Sundays in the forthcoming one year for wanderings. I had taken permission from my parents to travel wherever I want to. And for me, it was just like my passport. My wanderer's life started with a sudden opportunity to visit Nagpur which gave me experience a 45° C temperature in the month of June. As soon as the rainy season started in Mumbai, along with a few of my colleagues, we arranged the trek to Lohgad Fort & Visapur Fort near Lonavala in Maharashtra. It was a full moon in the sky that night. The trek was memorable because we selected only wrong turns while climbing down Visapur Fort. My college friends were forcing for a one Trek so we went to Tandulwadi Fort and had fun at beautiful Rainfall. Those days, one need cum responsibility was pushing me to travel for one more cause. That is the increasing rate in real estate was making us be aware of and to be to think about the future. In the month of August, I had a lonely trek at Brahmagiri in Nashik.

For Ganesh Festival in September, I spent 15 days at my village Tulas which is at Vengurla in Sindhudurga District. Here also, I continued my traveling and visited a palace at Sawantwadi near a beautiful Moti lake. I am telling you, there is full scope for photographers at Natural Port of Vengurla. Initially, Vengurla was a commercial center that was established during 1665 by Dutch traders and subsequently by British rulers. We enjoyed sceneries of the maximum possible area of the sea from the lighthouse.

To share with you, some of the Sundays were so unproductive and boring because it was difficult to get an affordable home whose seller will make you believe that he has all the required documents. In the month of December, it was an achievement for most of the trekkers to have a rich experience by reaching at top of a fort named Harishchandragad. The ultimate view of Sunset is famous from Harischandragad fort. In January month, we had trekked to a fort named 'Padar' near Bhimashankar and found it very tough. You need to do some rock climbing work to reach the walkway at the top. We had succeeded.

Ohh !!! I forgot to tell you about one important move. As I told you that I was in search of doing something interesting & memorable in life, I decided to go to the Himalayas. THE SAR PASS TREK.

In the months of May-June 2010, during my exam time, my colleagues went on the same trek. And after hearing their experience and watching some photos on an office computer, the first thing I ensured was that I am financially capable of going on this trek outside Maharashtra.

We did online Registration of the Youth Hostel

Association of India via their website. In March a small picnic was arranged on the ground of 'Mahuli Fort' with my college friends. This is the same spot where I did the first trek of my life on 1st July 2002 which actually enlarged my world. Eagerness was increasing with time continuously but it was the only test of my Patience.

My superior in office was changed & at the same time, it was time to apply for the leave. I was taking extra efforts to complete the task that was assigned to me before the target date. In my case the problem was getting leave approval to two subordinates from the same superior was a little challenging. My team leader had an opinion that if I could wait for this trek for the last year then I can easily wait for the next one more year. Every time while asking for a leave one came to know your importance at your office. The first time we were that much struggling for leave approval. The 'Sar Pass' trek was extending my reading time at night. I was reading all about the 'Sar Pass' trekking from all sources that I could. Those nights, I was playing the role of a clock for my parents. I wish I could read my engineering books with the same passion. For the 'Sar Pass' trek, everybody has to wear goggles for protecting the eyes from the reflected light from the snow. I don't like to wear goggles since it doesn't show you true colors of nature. But for the first time, I traveled a lot by wearing my first goggles. I found it necessary for traveling when again with my college friends I visited a Culaba fort. Again after some days, we visited a Panhala fort in Kolhapur on the bike. To increase my stamina, I was getting down one stop earlier from the bus or one stop later so that I could increase the walking distance to reach home. Since I was traveling a lot with others I could deny a day at the water resort in Virar with family on Sunday. It was the last week before my departure to Himalaya Trek.

And finally, we got our visa. Just kidding. Actually, we got our leaves approved by our boss. Those extra working hours helped us. I had bought Action shoes only for Trekking and I started using them much earlier so that I will be comfortable with those pairs. I bought 3 pairs of socks, 2 handkerchiefs, 1 hat from the local hawkers on the roadside at Bhandup as usual. My elder brother's friends who were with me at Padar fort gave me his trekking bag. We got binocular from one of our friends which were given to him by one of his friends. I carried my old T-shirts, pants which I was wearing only for treks. Thus I could lower my expenses other than expenses for traveling. Those days, during breakfast in the office our colleagues were getting bored because our talking was only about our childish wishes about travel. I still remember their reactions and expressions. Sometimes someone was pointing out any mishaps which could happen in our journey. Considering those changes of the calamity in our journey, I had prepared a cheque with my brother's name. I left my ATM card at home which was belonging to the account having the highest money balance. To be frank, I didn't want to grow up but I was not a child anymore.

A very important object which I should never forget at home is my Camera. A memory card of which was damaged during a picnic at a water resort. Just to get a memory card at the right price I visited so many shops. Finally, I bought it from a mall & I found it is very cheap at the mall comparing with small shops. Just to tell you, those days online shopping was not having that large scale which we are using now.

On Friday night, I started packing my bag & I realize how skillful this task is! How many shirts, pants, bedsheets, which is to wear while leaving home, what is to put in a bag at the bottom or top for frequent access? It was so confusing and repetitive. A face wash & sun cream were the new things at my home only because of this Himalaya trek. Some of my friends were teasing me that I should use that sun cream only to protect my existing dark complexion. Saturday, a half working day, was felt like so longer than usual full working days. There was no chance at all to carry tickets & printouts of youth hostels booking because I was continuously imagining that scenery. Those days also I was facing some medical issues. I was having an allergy to dust in the eyes, had surgery on the nose due to continuous painful sneezes. Even after so many deceases, I got a medical fitness certificate for the trekking easily but on the very last day.

After having a nice lunch at home, as usual, I was about to come out of the home. At the same time, my dad came earlier than usual from his work on a half-day leave especially for sending off me. I carried my heavy bag on my own since I had to carry it for the next 16 days, I convinced him not to come to the railway station just to carry the bag. As usual, I didn't pray, but I touched the feet of Mom & Dad for their blessings. I started my journey by giving two rupees to one Monk. I remember, one Monk said that I will be far away from my home for a longer time. For this statement Monk was not required. I was already going away from home for work and for traveling and anyway it was not a negative statement. If you want to do something great you must go beyond your limits.
I was feeling different that day while leaving home and

walking between alleys. Maybe I was the first person who was going to the Himalayas just for a journey. But I was a little worried about my family if I will not return from this adventure. Before my journey, I could only hear about the Himalayas when any couple was coming from Honeymoon. And nobody those couples ever used the word 'Himalaya'. For them it was only Shimla-kullu-manali. "Going for a trek?' was a usual question in the neighbor's face or to my ears after moving forward. Today this afternoon no one was out of the home. All were having a rest. But eventually, one friend known to me by face came in that alley and enquired about heavy sack & wished me for a happy journey.

I reached to local railway station by bus. Since my childhood, I have seen variety & progress in Railway tickets. But as usual, there was a long queue in front of one window out of four in Ticket house at Kanjur Marg. The coupon punching system that didn't require a queue was smartly being used by me. Why educated people and smartphone users don't use such an updated system and make a crowd is still a big question.

Since it was Saturday afternoon, the train was not crowded, but my sack has taken space of two persons which was bigger than allowed as per unwritten rules. Anyone, including me, could remember terrorist Ajmal Kasaab by looking at my getup. But most of the common men were looking steadily outside and were lost in their own problems. For them, they are so many passengers who regularly carry such weight daily.

For catching the express from Bandra Terminus, I changed my local train at Dadar. I still remember my first day at this station for the admission process of a diploma course in Mechanical engineering. Those days, after my school, I started traveling alone and I was not capable of catching a running train or getting down from the train in a rush. So, instead of getting down safely, I slipped on a platform. My sky blue-colored jeans got dirty.

For share Autorikshaw fair was only Rs.10/- & Rs.50/- otherwise. Already a fat man covered a huge space in one auto. Obviously, there was no minimum space for me with my bag. The auto driver suggested putting a bag beside the fat man allowing me to share the driver's seat. I condoned him by saying thanks & asked another driver.

This driver was in too hurrying. I was just waiting to see from which side he wants to through me out. I reached a Bandra Terminus & four more jokers cum trekkers came from the taxi. Amol, Vishal, Mukesh & Vinayak.

We were from the same office. I interacted with Amol during Nagpur's visit. Vishal was at Lohagad. Mukesh, Vinayak & Vishal together were with me on Panhalgad Fort at Kolhapur. Alphin & Ashwant, who were from the same office, were already waiting at the platform when we were waiting for them outside.

Garibrath Express, A name given to Express. In beginning, we were hiding the name of express, as it means a vehicle for the Poor. Is it indicates that you, citizens are poor and this mode of transport is for you? And this will be for you for so many years? I didn't like this name. But we were using this name for making fun too. This means we were imagining that everything in this train will have poor quality. One of the seats near the window was reserved & a person on the second seat near the window was about to come. I became the owner of charging points by putting the charger with the battery cells of the camera.

One family sat beside. One couple & one more lady should have to 'take care of their children but they were just 'handling' three children.

Just for a sake of passing the time, as soon as Vishal was about to get down from the train, it started by honking.

One lady with his son sat beside him unknowingly. We proved on the internet, which was available on Amol's mobile, that the seating arrangement was changed, but she was not at all ready to listen. In the end, the ticket examiner himself instructed her to leave our seats. She was already upset because her relative missed the same train.

I had made a call with mom informing her about the departure of the train at right time. Ashwant put out his camera from a bag & we started capturing photos of everyone.

In a very short time, a family beside us started requesting interchange seats. Already we were concerned about Amol & Vinayak, who was in another coach, changing their seat near us in our coach. While we were trying for them, someone only from us allowed them to change as they want.

Today's sunset was in Mumbai. We captured some images in cameras. Everyone was bantering on someone's style of work, way of eating, mannerism. We had snacks of bread-omelet. Mukesh was sleeping because last night he couldn't sleep just because of the imagination that he will at Himalaya after some days. Vishal was reading a book written by Ranjit Desai named 'Shrimaan Yogi' based on the life of King Shivaji. Alphin & Aswant started hearing songs on earphones. After some time, topics for discussion were finished within an hour. As it was started darkening outside, the frequency of looking outside the window was reduced. As you stop speaking with others and if your eyes are open, you start speaking with your soul about your past, your presence, your future, and your people and about you with your perception.

As decided, I wished to give complete rest to eyes at least during this journey. A few weeks before, I completed reading a biography of Charlie Chaplin, translated by Mr. B.D.Kher in Marathi. Till Friday, I was reading a novel written by Mr. Vishwas Patil named Mahanayak, the biography of Netaji Subhash Chandra Bose. His, India's Azaad Hind Sena was reached to Myanmar. Unlike Alphin & Aswant, I was not willing to hear songs also. I was avoiding earphones as I was feeling that music is continuously being played even there is no earphones. I started learning to handle Aswant's camera. Family Head besides me was reading a book.

Cursorily, I handle his book. He was about to give an exam for Civil Services, i.e. UPSC. He was from the state of Haryana as we identified from their language. I started turning pages as it was my favorite subject. A stone-age man, the empire of Saatvaahana, Chalukya, Rashtrkut, Mughal, and Mourya is part of the history of India & Maratha is a chapter on which I have read many books as my Mother's tongue is Marathi.

I found a mistake on the very first page & in the very first paragraph, that Chhatrapati Shivaji's father Shahaji left his wife Jijabai. Samartha Ramdas & Dadoji Kondadev were teachers of Chhatrapati Shivaji, which was also a wrong statement according to my reading. I have come to the conclusion that attempts to bring out correct information about Chhatrapati Shivaji are limited to one state of India, i. e. Maharashtra. But I am more concerned about a number of such books & a number of topics where wrong information is stored, conveyed to the number of its readers & is correction done or not.

After some time, one of the attendees came to give a pillow & blanket. He gave two blankets & a pillow for each. We gave him Rs. 150/-. He went by saying he will return Rs. 25/- afterward. I like to note down the amount because after some years the same price surprises us.

As soon we ordered a Veg dinner, immediately box having cold food was handed over to us. We convinced ourselves that this was a sign of why 'Garibrath' is called Poor Man's Express. None of us was so-called poor, but we have an opinion that everywhere poor are getting neglected. Anyway, at least the train was fully air-conditioned which cooled our head and that food also.

After some time, a Bogie started vibrating as speed increases. That's the reason while eating we were struggling to hold the food, especially liquid items was about to fall on the bed. For the same reason, Mukesh & Vishal avoid coming down for dinner & they had it at their upper berth only. After dinner, again we had some casual chit chat & our neighbors alarmed one more time to interchange the seat to sleep.

We allowed them. A man reading a history versus his Sister & wife together could not decide where to sleep. Now they were having so many options because of our acceptance for the adjustment of 5 seats. Their children were 'busy' playing, irritating Alphin especially. Some of us wanted to sleep at the earliest & some didn't want to wake up early morning because of children. A few moments later, the discussion got converted in the conference, I realized. Usually, there are two berths on one side of any express train, except this. In this train, there were three berths instead of two. Here we 'adjudicate' to sleep on these three berths. Two upper berths were already engaged. Finally, we succeed to grab our berths.

Some of the passengers were not having confirmed seats yet. They were expecting permission at least to sit on a floor or at least for a proper place, other than in front of the door, to keep their bags. Near to door, a space having partitions horizontally was empty, as pillows & blankets were removed. Somebody gave a small amount to the attendee to arrange the space for him as well as for his bag too but he occupied a large space, without thinking about other passengers who were outside, seated near the toilets. They were passing the taunts to attenders & these taunts were fallen into my ears since I was on the lower berth near the door. I was forced to hear those rude words of passengers seated near a toilet. Then, I realized that the glasses doors are not soundproof comparing with other express trains. A boy looking like our age group was sleeping for a long time, was awakened by the same attendee for returning Rs. 25/- only, though he could return that amount on the next day. The attendee went away without even saying an apology.

It was already midnight when I was fallen asleep, sensing the rhythm of my breath and the vibration of the train too.

Chalo Delhi

Sleeping is a boring action when your eyes are eager to see the Himalayas with your open eyes. So I woke up. Friends were already ordered tea. They were offering me too. I never liked having a tea without brushing my teeth & without splashing water over a face at least once, so I refused. "Have a bed-tea once; have you ever tasted in your life?" A question from the upper berth forced me to think. Anyway, I wished to do something new then I should also try these new things.

You have to do perfect balancing in moving train when you want to defecate, a very important daily natural routine. I praised a cup of Tea just to have a positive mindset because my body and mind need to make habit of any taste and temperature. We played songs on mobile on the loudspeaker.

By the time, our train reached Mathura Station we were started feeling so hungry. Someone was selling 'Pakoda'. We bought two plates of Pakodas containing 4 pieces for four of us. After one bite only Vinayak threw both. After 3 bites even I could not bear with it and threw those Pakoda in a dustbin.

We were standing on a platform near the train. One beggar, a lady, age near 60, started asking for money. I gave her a single coin of one rupee, which I was having at that moment. She started demanding for Rs.10/-. We asked her to return that one rupee and she returned it immediately. If someone watching this incident, he may be even wondering that that the beggar is really.

Train started. Now, we were waiting for two things only, the train journey should end at earliest & we should reach Delhi at earliest. That attender was sleeping outside near a washbasin. As he opened his eyes, I asked for Rs. 25/- with raised & loud voices intentionally. He wakes up in hurry & returned the money. For me, it was an act of sweet revenge for what he did yesterday with a passenger from Baroda. Have I the right to this revenge against his arrogant behavior? If yes, then someone else will behave with me in the same manner and it should be acceptable to me.

The train was reaching near to its last railway station. I asked the name of one pretty girl among those three shouting children. I don't remember her name but when I asked her surname, she replied that she doesn't have 'Sir'; she has her 'Madam'.

Finally, we reached Hazrat Nizamuddin Railway Station, which the last station of the train. 1st May 2011. I will always remember this day. At first, I made a call to Mom-Dad. It was 10 a.m.

As we started to walk on the bridge, cab drivers started pursuing. We kept walking. One of us asked for a rate just for curiosity & he assumed that we have already booked his cab. He followed us and also came from behind where we were having a Tea and trying to remove houseflies sat on our cups. Till the time, Amol was busy getting stitches to his bag.

We realized that we are on the wrong side of a bridge. So we again crossed the railway station. As we reached to another side one lady put a Flag of India, Tiranga, to my pocket near the chest. I felt proud and pleasant welcome. I guess she will ask for Rs. 2-3/- for that flag and I will offer Rs. 5/- but she asked for a donation. I asked for a purpose behind the donation. Then she started remembering & muttered and ended with "for poor children Sir". Putting a pointed pin to the flag is a crime; I informed her & returned that flag.

We came to the main bus stand near the Railway station. We were walking on a bridge to cross the highway. While stepping down, we saw a poor man, collecting a plastic bottle. We gave him empty bottles which we were having with us. He replied in English and with correct pronunciation, "Thank You". We wandered by his professional & formal reply. Laughing on our English we reached another bus stop. Some old, some new, some Air-Conditioned buses were passing in front of us. It was ISBT, i.e. Inter-State Bus Transport, from where we caught a bus which will drop us near India Gate. For this, we need to get down at the top of the Central Secretariat. Our actual site seeing in Delhi was started. We were the center of attraction in the buses of Delhi too because of hats, black goggles & big bags on the back. The bus started moving from behind the red Fort, Near Firozshah Kotla Stadium on a wider road than roads in Mumbai. After commonwealth Games, advertisements were kept as it was during games. Trees were given the shape of a mascot of commonwealth games.

This region of Delhi was similarly clean like a South Mumbai, but comparing with Mumbai, there were considerably fewer people even on Sunday. Not having shops on either side of roads, less frequency of signals, no potholes on roads were new things for Mumbai guys like us. We stepped down to the nearest bus stop for India Gate. It was an obvious comparison by us between Gateway of India & India Gate. Instantly photo session started. Boys of 10-15 years age group were swimming in black-greenish water. 'Rashtrapati Bhavan' can be seen at some distance. A soldier doing his duty was looking stronger than a gate. His walking style & keen glance could mesmerize anyone. Four soldiers & around the structure must be standing there for 24 hours. The right person at the right place at right time not only solves the problem but it prevents the problem from happening too. But I was guessing a number of monuments in India and how much soldier strength we are wasting at such monuments.

We started walking towards the Rashtrapati Bhavan. Some people were practicing Cricket in the net wearing helmets and pads. Most of the time, it feels that we play only this game and we are not giving importance to any other game other than cricket.

A journey started by AC bus again to reach Rajghat. Mahatma who did a great and hard effort for peace had a very peaceful place to live after the end of his life after living for others. Many children were playing in a garden near a trance of everyone's Bapu. Yes, there is anger for Gandhiji in some of the Indian minds, even today. After coming from a long distant place, even after coming to Rajghat, none of my friends came near to trance.

After spending 10 minutes we left the place. For me visiting the soldier and Rajghat was the start of a journey with the temple. We moved on to a way of the fresh room. Passing jokes & unnecessary comments, we reached near toilets. And at the same time, one young man from our age group & a lady between 35-40 ages came out from the same fresh room which was only for men. Our laughter was paused for a moment. Before going inside we turned back & at the same time, they were looking at us with a shameless smile. We forgot our last joke or whichever statement that time, so I am not able to remember it while writing this.

We filled up our bottles with cold drinking water & returned to ISBT by bus. Aswanth & Alphin returned to the bus stand after meeting their friends staying in Delhi. Rakes & Shreejith, who belong to the same working organization but in a different sector, joined us & thereafter a group of nine was formed. After entering the bus, it was a question who all will sit together when nine different seats were already reserved. A seat near the window was OK, but big sacks kept between legs were not giving a chance to move a leg by even a millimeter. We Indians have a habit of seating besides the person belonging to our language or locality or religion since our childhood. So there was the possibility of a group of 5 Marathi speakers & 4 Malayalam speakers may get formed, but involuntarily that did not happen. Those who were not having a reservation for a window seat & came in a group were sending others like us who were having a reservation for the window seat to another seat diplomatically by saying that "Seat anywhere, all of us will go the same destination."

The bus started & bags below the seat, between legs, started annoying. We were asking for artificial permission from a neighboring passenger, Vishal, to move a leg & he was also allowing dramatically since he was also waiting for the same deal. We started experiencing the warm air of Delhi. The rattling sound from window glass was ear-splitting than the actual Horn of the bus. Our engineering brain was awakening with ideas. We collected wrappers of bottles & a cap of the bottle and inserted those between two panels of the window for a tight fit. Windows went to sleep when we shouted that our Project has been completed successfully. We congratulated each other as it was a big achievement for us.

It was about 5 to 5:30 p.m. when the bus was stopped near a hotel. We went up on the top of the bus & tied our four big sacks by rope on the bus. If I would have come with my parents, they would have never given me chance to do this. Now we were feeling like a king and could drink packed orange juice sitting in our seats.

The bus started running on too long & further longer roads. We observed successive construction of bridges. The bus was taking big turns frequently because of the work in progress stage of roads. The bus had a stop at Haryana where people in a hotel were watching IPL, 20-20 match format of cricket. My interest was lowered to watch these cricket matches. I was not happy that players who were together and won the World cup will be against each other in the very next event.

Journey started. This time there were so many passengers standing in the bus, ready to go by standing only and were ready to stand for a longer duration. This is also a habit of Indians that they are ready to suffer but don't raise their voice for the improvement of facilities for which they pay taxes. Due to their way of speaking and language, the atmosphere changed suddenly. Aswant, who was in the process of learning the Hindi language, started singing Hindi songs. I was continuing the same songs when he was disturbing lyrics by mistake. We were not at all thinking about other passengers while we only were singing in a lower voice (according to us) in running the bus. But our friends only shouted to shut mouth & not to cry. We continued playing our all songs in our playlist & stopped later. We enjoyed a thick Dal-Roti & rice in a small hotel at 11:30 pm. We reduced the possible amount in a bill by sharing two plates among the four of us. We appreciated the quality of food to the hotel owner. He replied, "It's all about Customer Satisfaction sir" & forced me to recall my office. I conveyed this small conversation to friends & they started laughing. I shared that incident with a person who thanked me for giving me a plastic bottle in Delhi.

The bus was moving slowly where no street lights were installed beside those roads. I slept. Warmness in a bus was decreased considerably & started feeling chillness of breeze.

Love at First Sight

It was around 5-5:30 a.m. Cold pleasant air touched the corner of my eyelid. A large beautiful landscape running in the window frame replaced the splash of water for which I was used to early morning. Friends shouted & I had a glance at them also, scenes outside forced everyone to open their eyes fully.

The bus is also anxiously running to reach her destination along the bank of the singing river. Every small stone is adding a design to her beauty. A pure path of water flowing between wet and white stones, greenish yellowish trees beside the road and river were challenging every design produced by humans. It was a stage was set by the mountain and a river was walking on its own ramp.

A bus entered a beautiful dark tunnel. Lamps were looking like stars inside the tunnel and were having turns of the road. For us, it was like a ride in a park. Very soon, the first-ever mountain appeared covered with snow & we shouted from deep inside "wooooooo". We greatly realized that the place we selected is more beautiful than our imagination upcoming days will not be anything shorter than a dream.

From far-away a place, Mountain was appearing as it is decorated with ice & is shining proudly. There can't be anything more beautiful than this. Water was skipping from the way created by it whereas the bus was comparatively crawling in an opposite direction on a way created by someone else. A piece of natural melodious music by river water & an artificial sound by engine & rattling windows of bus together were playing an orchestra song to our ears. So, why does anyone will listen to a song over earphones?

After entering one of the villages, people started getting down from the bus at intermediate spots. A bus driver & conductor were in a great mood & hearing an old romantic song on a loudspeaker. We were shouting in between like Michael Jackson. I have a mad complaint about the human body that human eyes are too small to see this whole world. And will it be possible that the bus would be made of plastic or glass or any transparent material?

A woman behind my seat asked for a replacement of my seat near the window for Granny with her. As I told her I was traveling here for the first time Granny sat behind my seat. For a moment I was a little happy with my brain but very soon she alerted me by her statement that Granny may omit anytime. I ignored her trick and started looking outside by taking out my neck outside the window. Exactly at the same time, Granny started pushing forward that shutter of the window. The power was much enough to make me shout. Though I could make a sound to save me it was not audible to her. A woman stopped Granny. I came to know why they write a note on a bus not to put any of your part body outside the bus. A parade was going on at the military camp on another side of the river. After crossing some distance, we could see more and more people on road. Each of the houses was showing its own identity. Very soon, the bus reached a destination. We got down in a great hurry. Everyone was energetic and in a great mood. A mountain with a Snowcap is very near to eyes and travel agents & hotel agents were coming so closer to bags which were tied to the top of the bus. We removed our bags from the top quickly. A woman with a granny wished us for a happy & safe journey & went away with a promise to visit Manali if liked.

We decided to go to defecate in a public toilet near a bus stand. First time in life, we were going to use chilled water for all important natural activities. Needless to say, the Experience was like a self-torture.

We bought gloves & socks for the mountain climate in a nearer market. The cold environment here forced us to buy these items. My office colleagues suggested buying these items, but we decided to buy these items from here only since they are of better quality here, variety is more, and the cost is less. For us, it was appearing like 31st December immediately after 30th April. Rather, it was colder than 31st December than our experience in Mumbai. We had an inquiry at the counter, for a bus to reach directly to 'Kasol' but it was unavailable. A person from one of the private travels was trying to convince us that his bus goes directly to Kasol & bus which left the bus stand was the last bus. We couldn't believe that the timing of the last bus is early morning at 9:15 am? We informed this surprising information at the inquiry office. Then, both of them started doing quarrel. We escaped quietly & hired a four-wheeler. Till the driver gets ready, we had a heavy breakfast of Parathas in a hotel after cleaning a face and hand. Some of us used this time for shaving.

The journey started along with a new girlfriend, a river wherever she turns. Stones got a shape & design because of the impact and continuous flow of the water, making the river bank looking like a sari. A vehicle stopped by crossing the Bridge of Biyaas River. After a glimpse at the temple of ascetic Guru Vasishtha & surroundings, we were turning back towards the vehicle. Shopkeepers besides the roadside shops were requesting earnestly with love to see & touch 'Chingoo'. They were continuously saying that there are no charges to see 'Chingoo'. While taking an image of one shop, one of the sellers said I have taken a photo of 'Chingoo' itself. I thought going to a shop alone would be a time-wasting for others. Vishal & Rakes were going inside another shop. So, I joined them.

'Chingoo' is a type of Cashmere cloth. It is very very soft & available at this place only according to the seller. The keeper was ensuring us that this smooth cloth gives warmth in winter & gives a cooling effect in summer. That year, it has a cost of five to six thousand, and the seller was ready to give it in monthly installments and was ready to send it via courier. With a frank reply, we took permission from the shopkeeper without any shopping. I felt 'Chingoo' deserves appreciation & needs publicity. Nowadays I also see negative opinions about the same in social media.

We reached a temple of Hidimba & Ghatotkach; characters belong to the epic of Mahabharata. A vehicle parked near a garden. A teacher of an alphabet 'Y' that is 'Y for Yak' having shiny, plenty of white hairs were in front of eyes. Travelling gives you actual knowledge which you cannot get in books. If I did not decide to come here I would never realize the size of YAK. During my childhood, I was having an opinion that all animals are oh same size and equal to the size of the alphabet printed in my book. I was feeling an old relationship when I was moving a palm on his forehead. I was happy inside that he was accepting my love. I am so thankful for the education system in India, which at least introduced him in a book. Walking between the tall trees of Cypress, a thought came to mind that it should be called 'Skypress'. We reached the Hidimbadevi Temple. In a cave, everyone was telling there are footsteps of Mata Hidimba under a big stone. Crawling below the stone I touched those footsteps of a great mother of great Ghatotkach. But those were not footprints. It was the shape of footstep protruded above. I got confused. In India, we find so many temples with such shapes of stone and are published as an actual step of someone. We also don't find steps more than two at a particular place.

At the entrance of the garden, my friends were in a competition of hitting maximum bottles by a ball in a single attempt. It was a simple game of overarm bowling. There was a game of Archery nearer to balling. A person, giving this opportunity, was like a Guru Dronacharya, (a Guru of Ghatatkochas' Father i.e. Bhima.) His fees were Rs. 40/- for 8 attempts. Twice out of my eight attempts, an arrow penetrated the board somewhere. Practice makes man eligible to become better than today. Perfection is a limit. I practiced archery with 8 more attempts. This time, Dronacharya cajoled me, suggesting doing a career in this. I gave him Rs. 100/- happily. He too allowed me to try again twice for hitting an arrow & thrice for a ball. I followed a technique while playing with marbles while playing with a ball. Whatever you do in life doesn't go to waste. Practice doesn't make man perfect. It makes humans eligible to become better than today. Perfection is a limit that is to be crossed immediately after touching it. With thankful greetings, I left the school & moved to Bus stop in Manali again. This time, I had given rest to my eyes.

The vehicle reached a bus stop. After coaxing the same driver, we decided to go to Kasol with his vehicle. The cold journey started within the same cold & pleasant environment without having lunch.

2nd May, 6 pm, we had to report at the base camp of 'Youth Hostel Association of India' but first we reported to one restaurant.

Ordered some Parathas one after one then we visited one Artist's shop. His imagination was far away from our imagination, as it was reflecting from his paintings. I guess it needed deep and different thinking to understand his paintings. Everyone was describing it differently & he must be having a very unusual meaning of it. The cloth was painted with different fluorescent colors. When he enlightens his paintings by placing a light behind the cloth, the painting was looking more beautiful and surprising. I am unable to describe those in words. Background music, remix played by him, was so noisy for us, even if he played with lower volume. Overall; as an artist, his choice of songs, his paintings were different to have some opinion. But his paintings are definitely memorable.

Actually, for a restaurant, we crossed a Base camp. We returned on the same road. Near the downward steps, a bird having white feathers with a long tail crossed our group. He left the tree immediately, but it was a sign that binocular will be so helpful in this tour.

Stepped down the base camp, near 'registration 'tent". The

first group reached the day before, was listening to the rules & instructions. On the right side, there were so many mobile chargers charging the mobiles. There was a confusing mesh of wires confusing to identify which charger is connected to which mobile. Behind this arrangement on a posture, there were some images of birds that could be seen in this forest. I pointed to the bird which I had seen while descending.

Showing our own I-card, we got a separate I-card for our batch, named SP-2. These alphabets would keep our identity for a longer time. One form was given along with I-card. Due to habit in exams, we copied all the information by copying each other. Fortunately, we pasted our own photo. Tent No. 15 was allocated & two blankets were given to all of us.

By removing the socks-shoes, the leg started breathing with fresh air. Suddenly it became different dirty weather in a tent than outside, after removing of 18 socks together after using continuously for 3 days.

We completed important natural work by using water which was more chilled than Manali. After this, the next challenge was to have a bath with chilled water. It's indeed a Punishment. It was a need cum punishment to have a bath. We were not aware of the arrangement of the bath in the next few days; we were sure about not having the guts to have a bath after this.

For a longer period, I was wearing formal office wears & same in a night college. I wanted to see myself the way I was wearing during college. I wore a T-shirt purposely bought for this trek. It was its first day & friends were surprised after looking at me in this 'format' for the first time.

A spectacular mountain covered with snow was looking like a king sitting at the top. Different sounds of new whistles were ensuring a free exhibition of unseen birds. The first group, i.e. SP-1, was playing volleyball on the ground. An arrangement of bulbs for the campfire was placed. Considering air pollution & global warming, burning down wood, playing music on a speaker, smoking, putting up a fire, such harmful activities for nature were prohibited. A cultural event was about to begin by the SP-1 group.

A field director & his associates sat at the front row facing the audience. An anchor of the show forced each of his batchmates for some performance. But everyone was shouting with someone's name. None was ready. Mithun Das, a camp leader, forced one of them to come ahead. As he started to sing, others started clapping deliberately to stop him. One camp leader sang a song, originally sung by

Mohammad Rafi. All appreciated him. One singer started to sing one Marathi song violating lyrics so badly. My friends were forcing me to perform something. Initially, I was having doubt that they will treat me the same as they were clapping to the bad singers. Even I wished to sing the same song which lyric was disturbed by the earlier singer. I decided to sing the same song properly. Since it was not the competition, I changed the song after reaching to front.

The day before, 1st May it was Maharashtra Day. I sang my State Song on this occasion & luckily public became listeners & chorus too. I was thankful for a good response.

I was in a line for my first cup of Bournvita in life. I bought this cup for which I want to utensil shop for the first time. It was a strict instruction by superiors to wake up at 6 a.m. sharp. Accordingly, lamps in all tents were allowed to glow until 10 p.m. Sharp.

Best Camp - a Base Camp

The second day in a camp, 3rd May. It started with a first bed-Tea in a life. After completing all-important work, our batch was on the ground at 6:30 pm. The camp leader was whistling repeatedly & loudly. Many guys were too late. The field director questioned everyone for disobeying the instructions. He repeated that we were for a disciplined trek not for a picnic. We, Sp-1 & SP-2, around 90 trekkers went to the ground for an exercise. After a considerable break for an exercise at the gym, it was a little unbearable. Everyone liked laughter therapy. It is not taught by anyone, I am doing this since birth. Everyone forgot the pain after having laughter therapy. SP-1 batch got separated and instructed to go for the training of Rock climbing & Rapling. And we went for a small trek for acclimatization.

A separate red trekking sack for an individual was issued. Now I could be less conscious while placing the bag anywhere. After walking for 30-40 minutes over a slope, we, 47 trekkers, halt at one point. Automatically, five groups were created while sitting at a particular place. Those, who were already with a group sat separately & those who came alone joined any group. The camp leader ordered to play Antakshari between 5 groups.

And I started to sing aloud. After a long time as it was having an opportunity. Someone started to sing songs in Malayalam, as the stock of Hindi songs was fallen short. We also reacted to Marathi's song. Because of songs, it was easy to identify someone's mother tongue as well as the quality of singing. There was a minimum of 15 trekkers from Maharashtra as well as from Karnataka. Some were from Delhi, Rajasthan & some from Gujarat. Karnataka group was looking more excited. Maybe they had an extra cup of bournvita yesterday. They were in identical dress. Software engineers working in the same organization were seated separately. After some time, we could rememer the faces of our SP-2 batch mates.

While refusing someone's song or continuing crazily his song we were giggling unnecessarily. So our group members got attention and could start remembering us. Some of them might have thought that we are rogue. Descending the journey was a little slippery towards the base camp which was required as practice.

All gathered near a stream of Parvati River. There was a supply of water through pipes when we had the first bath at the camp. Now we were about to enjoy an actual temperature of chilled water.

Avoiding slippery marbles we reached to big stones and touched a finger point to water. Haah….A freezer should be shameful. It was not chilling. It was thrilling water. It required genuine courage to insert hands in water and splash it over a face. However, we attempted deliberately to understand our capability of sensing such temperature by standing in cold water. We came here to do such different things. But no one could stand for more than 10 seconds. We started the photo session by sitting funnily on stones like models on the calendar. Some sat peacefully in the shadow of a tree & lied down on a big stone. I was also an isolated man on an isolated island, watching an umbrella of Cypress…sky press tree. Trees on the other side were tilted to our side to watch their children. After a longer period, we could her pleasant sound of peace. For half an hour there was no movement at earth.

A long whistle disturbed everyone. We were in love with a new girlfriend, the river. As an order given by the camp leader, we immediately started 'searching' the garbage, plastic especially. For us searching for an inventor of plastic was important. We wanted to fight with him. But at the same time, it was a lesson for everyone that we users are polluting the world. And anyway, all the garbage was put in the plastic bag itself. So we canceled our plan of a fight. After half an hour, we reached base camp. It was an orientation session in the evening. The field director explained 'YHAI' in detail. We were already having respect for the organization. Everyone started introducing himself as per instructions and announced his name, occupation & number of camps with YHAI only.

The field director expressed his usual opinion about groups. There was the formation of a group just like us. People from the same company or of the same language or the same state were creating a group and behaving like a separate batch. He wanted to be here with the condition to forget an individual's designation.

Mr. Rathore was appointed as a group leader, he introduced himself in Gujarathi language & he was on his fourth camp with YHAI. It was considered that he is familiar with the rules of YHAI. At the same time, due to a giant personality, and with the hopes of people may afraid, Kapil was selected as vice Group Leader. Now, it was time to decide environment leader. A girl in front of the Field Director was selected because of a caption return on her Nike T-shirt, which was 'Just do it.

Already we were on a leave from the office. We had a sigh as we avoided having the responsibility of doing any work.

But, today evening we were ready to have a responsibility of campfire & decided to rock the party. Group Leader Mr. Rathore, had to schedule the program. We heard a whistle from somewhere was for a dinner. Kapil came with an expectation of a minimum of two performances from our group, where we were having dinner at a corner of the ground. We promised my individual performance, a group song in Marathi & one song in Malayalam. I wanted to sing very first but I will announce my song on stage only. Just to save the time, next announcement for the group song will be announced by me, Kapil instructed.

A long whistle & a previous batch SP-1, our SP-2 & some from SP-3, SP-4; around 100 persons were in front of the electric campfire. The field director (FD) & his assistant sited on respective chairs. FD shouted "Fire, Fire" and we continued loudly, "Camp Fire".

This jubilation happened twice. He welcomed new

joiners at camp & instructed for the next day. Surprisingly, our main group leader was in great sleep.

The program started by an anchor named Anushri. After a prayer in Sanskrit, she announced my name. I heard clearly "Thank you" when I dedicated the song to the audience & started to sing a motivational song from Hindi Movie 'Lakshya' that song was "Lakshya to har haal me Paana Hai ". Selection of the song matched Vishal's suggestion. The audience responded nicely after hearing the song. I called my four Marathi Friends, Kapil & advocate Patil. We, a total of 7, so-called singers, sang a Marathi Song.

Mr. Kamat, age around 50 Years, shared some jokes with attempted Hindi. Those were hilarious while hearing known jokes in a different version of Hindi. You should enjoy a style of speaking also. A group from Bengaluru came forward & started a ballet.

One man stood in the middle and did not have a movement for some seconds. Another person started showing an action of striking on stone with a hammer & chisel. He made a statue of Lord Krishna from that stone. He prayed by joining his palms, & representing himself to the Hindu religion. As he left, the third person started changing the shape of the stone & converted it as both palms of a man were in front of face heading upward. The posture was representing Muslims. The next man came & converted the statue into a statue of Christ. Hindu & Muslim was passing by that statue and started doing quarrel with "Catholics" by looking at the statue. Now one more guy came ahead, converted the same statue in the posture of Mahatma Gandhi & messaged through a mime act that we all are the same.

Literally, everyone appreciated clapping loudly. Again

one man from the Bengaluru group came forward to draw a picture. Vasant Rao was reading a list of his achievements while he was sketching. It took 10 to 15 minutes to read a whole list when an artist was drawing a picture with curves & strokes. Without a mistake, he drew a lord, Ganesh. All praised him by claps. He gifted that sketch to YHAI.

With two consecutive performances, everyone was happy and in a great mood, including us. But we wanted to have an impact on our group in the program. I requested Kapil for one more performance while F.D. was giving a speech. Kapil himself canceled his song & told Anushri to declare my name. I performed mimicry of Sir Sachin Tendulkar & some Bollywood stars. It was a successful show and was appreciated by all. Program over and immediately there was a long queue for bournvita. My group appreciated my performance as usual but new friends from the same organization were surprised and happy. A lamp switched off at sharp 10 p.m. When we entered a tent, four more trekkers were already in a tent and occupied space more than required. Obviously, they were not moving at all. As we are friends, we slept with a very small gap between us sharing warmth with one another. A day ended.

4th May 2011. The day started at 5 a.m. Bed tea is the first activity. No one has the courage to bathe after the chilled experience at the river the day before & a thrilling bath on the first day here. That repeated whistle started irritating, forcing all to hurry unwillingly. Today again we are on the same ground for an exercise. Today again there is an increase in the population of our small YHAI country. Today an exercise with overenthusiasm on the earlier days has affected the body, making each movement half or incomplete. Today, we, SP-2 are about to go for rock-climbing & rappelling. SP-1 was about to go for the main trek & SP-3 for the small trek. At 9 a.m. SP -2 returned to Base camp. I took a camera only & stopped at boulder having different patches on it. This black stone was suitable for practice as per my experience. One, from YHAI, started his practical lecture.

He tied up a rope with a proper knot at the top of the

stone. One decided to be seated there. Putting a belt another one started showing movements to do & to avoid. He was teaching where to put palm, fingers, toe, how much force is needed for how much time or moments. He was showing how one may get hurt due to some mistake or how to correct to the right move after mistake. He was showing all these stunts and mistakes without falling. We realized the importance of the rope and knot.

It was looking difficult when he climbed up on a flat portion of stone at the upper portion of the rock. One after one, we started rock climbing. We were not in a hurry at all. A queue formed by 10-12 trekkers. All other stones were resting on stones. After 5-6 boys, everyone clapped especially for a girl 'Harini'.

Some climbed up properly, some fallen in between. Some were standing below and were only giving a variety of suggestions for caution to one who is climbing. Repetition of their jokes was so boring. As everyone guessed, those advisors were falling from the first level to the end. It is easy to advise than to implement in practice. They spent too much time like that 100-meter patch was like 1000 meters.

Now, it's my turn. I moved forward keeping a goggle. I gave a signal loudly, "I am coming." I climbed up 3-4 patches simply. The next portion was so flat & vertical. As I started moving up, the person sat above pulled me up. This way he has reduced overall time for training. I captured images of different moves of my friends in my camera from the top when they were climbing. The person who sat beside me got bored after pulling 50 climbers without having a break. The day before 6-7 guys from the SP-1 batch only did this activity. A trainer beside me told me that the SP-2 batch is better and looked excited since many guys participated. After rock climbing, he showed a practical of rappelling which was simpler. I went to the top of the same rock from the backside. After wearing a helmet & tighten the belt rappelling was easier as experienced by everyone.

A cool drink was getting prepared on the ground. Captain Rathore & Kapil were giving drinks to all. They were calling each one again & again because the quantity of the cool drink was too plenty to finish. We were going away from drinks because the bucket was about to finish and the one who will take the last drink from the bucket will have to carry that bucket to the base camp. As I told you, we were not willing to do any small work. But Amol carried it. A pleasant rain started unexpectedly while returning to base camp. This was the special rain without season, comparing with rain which created problems in Mumbai. We were experiencing winter at Manali after summer in Delhi & now rain in the winter season. Overall, we experienced 3 seasons in 3 consecutive days. All reached base camp with wet clothes. Most of the mates were thinking about how to spend their leisure time. As I started shaving as soon as I could share the small frame of mirror with 2-3 persons (with their own blade though).

I had a worse experience with the batteries of the camera. Every time we consume batteries at the beginning of the journey and later it becomes useless when we require it actually. Zero battery lowers values of the whole camera to zero, as experienced. But this time I was ready with precaution. Charging all batteries was the most important activity. It was decided already to grab each important moment in the trek. We saw arrangements for battery charging at the entrance near the stairs & 3 to 4 boys were keeping a close watch. It was special attention to the charging of batteries than mobile. Assuming unavailability of electricity for next 7-8 days in a journey; we were so careful.

There were 4-5 switchboard panels on a single bench. Each point was busy with some connection. 16 Out of about 150 were getting an opportunity to charge their instrument. It was a risk to leave the connection & move away. Not because of the worry that someone may steal it but if anyone may remove the connection for his cause.

I was having a charger that charges two batteries at a time. Just to save time, I requested Rakes for his charger which charges 4 batteries; but it was not working properly. It required a minimum of 8 hours to charge any battery completely, so it was not possible for any of us to have a watch there for a longer period. We decided our shifts. By connecting three plugs to four connections we created a tower-like arrangement to charge many mobiles and chargers of the camera. I guess this is the only subject where YHAI to improve about safety where switchboard gets high load.

"Whose connection is this?" someone entered in a tent near the group & in front of everyone, he removed a pin. We declared him as our target to harass. It was quite irritating while hearing him his explanation and anything. He also had a quarrel with Vishal in beginning. We were not cooperating with him for any activity & any comment. Only once, we agreed to him unwillingly, when he was having an argument about the color of the bulb i.e. a green or yellow!!!

In the evening, it was Sp-3 who has to perform in a

campfire. After dinner at 8 o'clock, everyone sat on the ground. The very first statement by an anchor was, they were not having a single performance. He requested other groups. Some members from his batch were shouting with the names of others. After hearing those names, without knowing them personally, we were also shouting with the same names. One could not sing even two lines with proper lyrics and then forget about the rhythm also. After some noisy minutes, one boy & girl, from Gujarat, came forward with some pre-decided performance. They started dancing with singing. A girl started moving around the campfire, but maybe it was not planned properly; the boy started moving around the public. It was looking like he was going outside the ground while performing Dandiya. Finally, he stopped when the song stopped. Maybe they were trying to involve everyone in dance. We noted and were happy that our performance last night was better. F.D. declared our next movement for the main trek on the next day. A day ended with Bournvita. It was 10 p.m.

Get-Set-Go

5th May. Can someone stop that irritating whistles? Everyone was ready at 5:30 am. We forgot that we have a Bath daily. After an exercise on the ground, we started preparing our Red rucksack provided by YHAI, especially for the trek. I put maximum objects brought from home, which I could carry. One of the volunteers checked the weight of my sack & instructed me to show all essential things which I put in the Red sack.

Snacks weighing 250gms, brought from home, kept away after the hard decision. One out of two bottles each of 1.5 liters, removed. A cargo pant, which was obtained after a lot of search in so many shops, decided to carry. Soap kept away in my bag, as soap paper is lighter in weight & easy to carry in the pocket. A wallet was not required at all. As there was the least chance of network availability, I kept my mobile, in my own bag. I had a plan to keep my beard in a different style every day, but I forgot the mirror at home & canceled my plan. The arrangement of blankets done by YHAI at every halt and the quality of the blanket were better. So bedsheet having less thickness but the big thickness of love kept in my green bag. I was carrying the same blanket for every outing but I must think practical. A t-shirt of a different look & half-pant rested in a bag. Inspector was not satisfied after this huge sacrifice. And going further without some very important & special things objects was like a tour without friends.

Camera, a first companion. After having a trek at 10-12 forts without a camera in Maharashtra, after looking at my own photos in someone's camera 5-6 times, after knowing some skills & after some learning from others I bought Point-and-shoot camera. Since that time, a journey without a camera was an offense like traveling by train without a proper ticket. A binocular was a necklace given by someone with which we could prance. Often I found it important to have it at home so that I could observe whenever Mars, Saturn, the moon come closer to earth. It was one of my favorite subjects during school days which I am missing since I joined Engineering.

On condition that a binocular will be carried by 5-6 of us alternately we were permitted. I wore a jacket & put on a cap & did showiness about a weight reduction. I was relieved when I was convinced of my capability of carrying this much weight. It was a rule not to carry a bag weighing more than approx. 5 kg.

A steel plate having 4 partitions; found at the home; put in a red bag. A Tiffin box was must require carrying the lunch while moving from one camp to the next. It created a problem at home when I carried my father's tiffin box which they carry daily. Such an incident was happening 6 years after leaving the college, VJTI. I did not even think about detergent or soap is required to wash these. Dad bought a bottle of hair oil bigger than required since that moment only I was imagining leakage of oil from a bag. The cheapest socks, as there will not be hesitation at all to while throwing it after use, were in a red bag. I recalled I was fighting with my elder brother for use of each other socks by mistake, because of the same uniform in the same school. A chain to lock the bag & another for self-defense was not required during the trek. An old thick sweater of favorite sky blue color was important to wear. Thermal wear was a new kind for me, came to know at this place only and carried it in a bag.

It was my dad's duty to pack our bags for any tour. I was missing him a lot on that day.

I kept my own bag in the storeroom. And put a bag at my back which is needed to carry for the main trek. Two parallel lines were formed by people of SP-3, SP-4 & SP-5 till the stairs. We had to walk between these lines.

A long whistle. A queue of boys started walking behind the girls. It was not new for us. Trekkers in a line were clapping in a rhythm for motivating us and to say goodbye to us. We felt like a star. Everyone might be feeling like a hero. Many audiences will know me because of my mimicry performance and they will not forget it easily, is my modest opinion about myself, as usual. A hairy dog also started walking with us. One fellow was missing in our group. He wanted to go with the previous batch, SP-1, as one of his friends, was in that batch. He left our batch since he was not permitted. I don't think such a decision is required when you are with YHAI and with nature. But in another way, it was a good sign that a person with such a nature will not be with us for upcoming days.

All of SP-2 waited for the last person ascending upstairs. I captured a photo of the whole group after running ahead. A journey started in a forest after crossing a concrete bridge. We started walking parallel to the river. Just after few minutes, I had a Hi-Fi with the boulder where we had training of rock-climbing. This is the first time we were walking with heavy bags on the back, containing the weight of Tiffin & of a 1.5-liter water bottle. Many, including myself, felt tired. As soon as I sat under a tree, Kapil a giant reminded the instruction not to sit in a way & I reacted, of course. It was looking like I was sat only when I was in front of him.

A walk begins immediately. As usual, my speed lowered. After few steps, I put my jacket wore a jacket to show the reduced weight of the bag at camp and removed the binocular for the first time. I was walking along the river, looking at a mountain continuously, peacefully, lonely. Someone was crossing me & moving ahead. I was ahead of someone if he is waiting for friends or was separated for urination. It was not my experience only; there were a few others also like me.

A foamy river, a variety of different sounds by birds, tallish Cypress trees, trees with colorful flowers & cool air were everyone's companions. We were started feeling cold if we stopped walking & it was also a prestigious matter if more trekkers go ahead of us. Though trekking is not a competition, walking continuously maximum is a must satisfy our ego. I could barely see others for few seconds because of successive turns, slopes & trees. A narrow way only was showing the small way ahead. Arrows were painted with limestones on rocks in the right place for us to understand the direction.

As I started feeling lonely, a narrow way suddenly turned into a wide cotton road. Giant goats were having their breakfast, lunch with their young ones. Some were looking aged. Goats having annular horns were looking more attractive. Some goats were having shiny hairs like they put on some dye. These must be from metro cities, hiding their true colors under the artificial color and not satisfied with color gifted by nature.

I was feeling so jealous while they were enjoying natural food without any extra effort. If we compare them with human beings, we wait for rain or arrange an irrigation water supply, will depend on farmers to harvest painstakingly, and then forget that pain, then forgets the farmer too and at the end find so many mistakes in the food served to you. We expect variety in lunch & dinner every day. We avoid repeating one item in a week. It's good than a week contains only 7 days. We have a variety of non-veg food, especially in fishes. Being from Konkan as origin we have a good frequency of fish; but, hey, why we are talking about fish? Fish in a week is my weak point. I will not write……..sorry.

Yes, making a way between white goats, playing with them, and attempting mimicry of their voice continued walking. A goatherd rested calmly under a tree, was having plenty & dark black haired dog. None was with him as a company. He was alone too! We reached Lunch point. All were on a longer mat. Tired, done, and dusted.

We haw do many packets of biscuits, wafers, noodles & stove. One villager with his mobile shop sat on the ground. Tired & hungry trekkers ordered noodles, bread-omelet, etc. We also rested near a big stone. As I rested keeping ahead on my bag, I heard a little sound of some damage. I was afraid of the breakage of goggles. I removed a goggle in a great hurry from a cover. The only plastic cover was broken, saved a goggle & lowered my worry.

Obviously, it would be time-consuming for him to make any item for 46 hungry trekkers. Within that period, we could go much ahead, decided by all 9 of us. We continued walking after informing others. I started feeling tired after jumping over the stones while crossing some streams. Someone was passing a rumor that after half an hour we will be reaching to next camp. We were passing the same message since it is a common idea in any trek for increasing patience. This half an hour was increasing to one hour after every half an hour. After crossing so many slopes, ups & downs, we met a boy, 6-7 years old. He informed me and Vishal about his school too. There were a total of 14 students in his class. A school was for girls too. We had a little chit-chat with him. Vishal put a goggle on his dreamy eyes & shown him his photo. He pleased after looking at himself with a stylish goggle. A journey of 15-15 minutes started again.

A day in a Happy Village

As mentioned in the trekking map after walking approximately 9 km we reached a village named 'Grahan'. As soon as, I did a salute to children breathlessly, they were replying with a smile and salute. Some of them were waving hands with Chuckle. Receptionists in the office should have trained here from local ladies to welcome someone with a smile. I always have got confused about why we make females sit at the entrance of offices? Means, though we are talking about women rights at one side; are we using them as an attractive object to feel our guest happy?

One lady was keeping watch on her cows, looking down in a valley. She had a farm on this mountain! It was so surprising that human has divided even a mountain into their portions! How difficult it was to count how many such portions exist on earth!

She had so many questions about Mumbai's life and it was luxurious according to her. She & many like her are waiting at many villages for facilities & relaxed life. She has no idea that people in cities are excepting more facilities, equal facilities, and facilities during the work in progress while everyone working for facilities & also wish to have simple life like her, away from facilities. We were encouraging each other for lifestyle. Coming to the topic, she encouraged the current situation that our tents were at a distance of about 10 minutes. We assured her about our visit to her home. Those 10 minutes were again half an hour for our tired legs.

At around 1:30 p.m. boys in a sweater, playing cricket with a season ball in the flat ground in front of the colorful temple. The popularity of cricket has reached every corner of India with every hit in every match. It is the only game customized everywhere as per available space & equipment. There was a handloom in almost every house, where anyone could turn his head because of the systematic arrangement of colorful threads. Their clothes were as colorful as colorful birds. Most of the women were busy weaving without looking at needles with the speed of robots.

I was capturing a photo of a mother who was bathing his baby. He stopped suddenly when his mother told him about us. More villagers were looking out of the casement.

It's pleasant to experience when a village greets you when you have done nothing for none.

Tents erected for one month were waiting for us & could be seen from one point. This time we were actually about to reach within 10 minutes. Friends were having lunch beside a stream of water sited on stones. We crossed a river & went up the smaller slope. Camp leader Mr. Vivek Khole was waiting for everyone & welcomed us.

Amol & friends reserved a separate tent for our group. So, instead of going inside a tent, I kept a bag under a tree to make her rest. It was feeling heavier with the time after carrying it continuously on the shoulder. Friends were having lunch together sitting on the broken horizontal trunk of Cypress. I opened my Tiffin having chapatti with chickpeas & feeling satisfied after every bite. In fact, only a first bite was enough for mind and tongue; the remaining was for the requirement of the body. I ate 6 to 7 chapatis easily. Mr. Khole came for a chat. He was our camp leader at Grahan. A doctor, in our group, from Gujarat, came first & reached at 1:00 pm sharp, Mr. Khole informed. I guess it was Doctor's clinic time.

Within this time a flexible tube was connected from the river & relieved in the bucket near to camp. After pouring chilled water in a body, I entered with a refreshed mood in a new tent.

"May I come in Sir, "I requested officially.

Everyone replied instantly, "No, No".

A new gentleman Mr. Suhas Natu, from Nashik joined us in our tent. Everyone was having a rest in their respective tent & we were having a chat with Mr. Khole. Sir keeping his old diary in front of him started singing parody songs. Music was stolen from any Bollywood or

Marathi movies & the lyrics were so hilarious. Just after 2-3 songs, we had a tea break at the show started again.

In the beginning, Vinayak, Amol, Vishal, Mukesh, Natu uncle & sir were in a show. After some time it became a concert & those who understand Marathi joined us. I was thinking that only Bollywood stars sing and dance at beautiful places. But, I was singing my favorite songs in the beautiful nature of the Himalayas.

In the concerto, I sang a song that we used as a pray in a secondary school. Devotional songs, romantic songs, sad songs, friendship songs are frozen suddenly at the tip of the tongue as someone called Mr. Khole for an urgent decision. Being a Camp leader, he had other priorities. While singing we were not aware that 3 beautiful school girls were singing local songs beautifully at some distance in front of tents and Bengaluru group & some trekkers were listening to them. Instead of singing, we should encourage local talents.

A mountain at four sides, tents at the middle of green meadow together were looking like a separated island. A home visible at far distance in a village & a camp here had a borderline of 12 feet Wide River; three sides were covered with long Cypress trees. A mountain having a mantle of snow was far away & looking giant. I wished my home should have such surroundings and I recalled that I need to a pending task of searching for a new home.
Someone gave a hint that our batch had to stay for a day in this village as the weather is not good enough at the next camp. No matter, we decided to have a rest today & to wander about in Grahan village the next day.

It was evening time. A network for mobile was available at a particular spot in a village. After a 10-15 minutes' walk, we returned back to the village again. I had already kept my mobile in a bag at base camp. A network was available at the exact corner of one shop & at a corner of another closed house. We could get range could if mobile was kept at a particular height at a particular angle only. Everyone was missing the range as he was moving the handset down and keeping it in loudspeaker mode to make a voice audible. Alphin & Aswant were waiting for the network near the shop for a longer time. Amol & Vinayak were showing their skills by keeping mobile in one hand & taking the support of pillar by another hand. Both were standing on 2-3 fingers of a leg. I captured those funny postures on my camera. I was just waiting for the successful attempt by any of them so that I can speak with my mother. 2-3 school girls were hopping in the cricket ground. Electric wires over homes were disturbing the beauty of possible frames for my camera. I asked one boy for a bat & ball, he went hurriedly but did not come.

For a longer period, everyone was in some position. I had a small conversation with my mother after Vinayak. The first sentence was common by both of us that conversation may get stopped suddenly. An old villager came near a shop. He took his handset in a right hand, dialed a number, talked with a normal voice, ended a call by himself & went back. It took an overall maximum of 2 minutes for him. We, having an ego about our engineering degree, had felt it like a slap by this person and were quiet for some seconds. We had a disdainful glance at each other & laughed for 5 minutes. We enjoyed that insulting miracle.

I recalled one television advertisement published by Favicol at that time. One old person put out bait in the water to hook a fish & gets bored after waiting for a longer time. One villager reaches the same shore by singing a song. He puts four drops of Fevicol adhesive on a stick and dips that stick to water. Fishes get caught quickly to the stick. So, the first elder person feels ashamed and keeps watching him surprisingly. I told about this commercial to my friends & the whole incident to Vishal, Mukesh and Rakes met us while returning to the camp after 1-1.5 hours.

The camp leader announced our batch to stay at the camp for an extra day. Due to poor weather conditions or due to required material had not reached the camp whatever reason behind it we did not have any concern for any reason. We were already feeling satisfied with the current surrounding on this first day itself. Sir told different directions to defecate.

Along with Amol, I left with colorful tissue papers and soap papers. It was evening time. We were instructed to go away maximum from camp. A way between grasses towards the river was muddy and was having a slope. It was difficult to find the correct place. It was looking like we were on-site survey. A very simple place, people had left signs, or as we decided to finalize any place someone was shouting to go ahead.

After doing the important activity, we ascended again towards the way between grasses. It was dark by the time we reached the camp. Dinner time was about to start. We had steaming food but it was a dilemma about washing the utensils because touching that cold water was like punishment. Skin and bones were getting numbed. We were wearing hand gloves immediately after cleaning hands. Wherever we found an opportunity we kept our feet in cold water causing a crack in both heels. A part near the heel was paining and resulted in the reduction of walking speed. We released our socks to play into the fresh air. Otherwise, they could suffocate us and take revenge for making them suffocate for a longer time. Shoes were getting shivering outside.

We tied one rope at top of three bamboos in a tent and kept our clothes to make dry and tied one torch. Not to get bored and after having permission we removed 4 packs of playing cards and started playing. We were about to stop playing when sir requested to enter our tent, he allowed us to continue. Sir started singing his parody songs. While playing cards we were also singing Hindi Classics. After some time it became a studio. We started singing maximum stanzas in a song whichever we could recall till 10 p.m. We ended with a tribute to Kishor Kumar, Mohd. Rafi and stopped our concert just to make other sleep. We were playing cards in the light of a rechargeable torch and not getting bored at all. We just decided to sleep because we sleep at night.

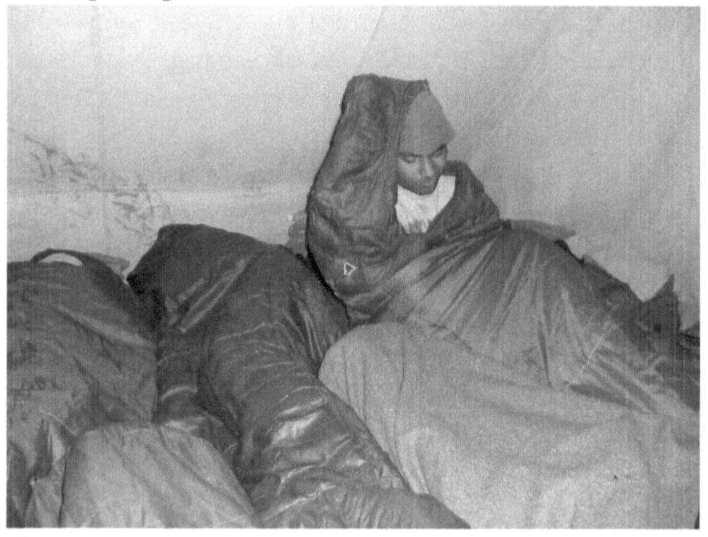

 Sleeping bags were an issue for us at this camp. I was handling that soft, lightweight, and easy-to-carry bag for the first time. Its length was about 5.5 Feet like made especially for me. I positioned it flat and entered. After everyone entered in their individual colorful bags everyone was looking like an insect. I was a little confused about the top portion of the bag. It is to be taken at the face from the front or from the back? I kept it open and went inside further. Water bottles were filled. Batteries in torch carried while leaving home were ended. I carried two extra cells but I couldn't find one. So my torch was useless. I ensured Amol about the location of his torch. I was sleeping near the door of a tent. So there was a possibility of feeling colder, but in a Sleeping bag, no one felt cold.

 It was 2 p.m. at midnight. Taking a torch I decided to

go to pee. Amol had tied the knots of the door. I was having an emergency. I could untie the bottommost knot and started crawling to come outside. So the dog came with us from the base camp and a dog in a village started barking. I reversed myself immediately and decided to reach the other door of a tent. It was difficult to identify 16 legs of 8 people who were in a sleeping bag. I was just guessing and finding the place for afoot. A torch was with me only. I reached that door with half-opened eyes, crossing one or three legs and balancing myself on a slippery sleeping bag. Knots were tied here also. I was not having enough time. Untied the last knot and came immediately after confirming there is no dog nearby. Done it!! I looked at the sky as a habit and saw plenty of twinkling stars. It was incomparable.

It is the richest form of the sky. Each star was showing its own presence. A moon was clear with his dark spots. Anyway, we see negative marks of someone close to us and meet us regularly. The whole world was sleeping except me. I did robbery of so many stars without making aware to any dog. The robber went inside with fear of dogs. I closed my eyes just because my body needed complete rest.

A day dawned. We couldn't recollect the day and time which was not required at all. Human has tied watch on his wrist or watch has tied him in restrictions that are to think of. Time has started deciding what is to be done by you at which time. Humans are not living a day completely and unaware about the next day have started putting a calendar and just pressurizing themselves unnecessarily.

Sun rose. All livings started their activities. A day started with most of the unnecessary activities. I had a bed-tea just to increase the amount of water in my body. I brushed my teeth with unnecessary toothbrushes and toothpaste. The use of a stick of neem tree for cleaning teeth is our ancestral activity. We were already freshening up only by the view of our surroundings but, still for formality, we splashed that cold water from the pipe on our faces. The temperature was about 1 or 2 degrees Celsius. I came to the senses after taking that cold water in cupped palms. Though we were having an experience that it needs guts to touch the water we were forgetting that somehow. I splashed water cautiously. We once again started searching for a suitable place to defecate. Since there were no toilets available, we have to do open defecation. A day before, we had visited some locations but did not like any plot. Now that plot was looking like people sat in the ground for a strike. Avoiding the exact subject one was asking only "have you done?"

This day was dedicated only to the rest. There was heavy rain at the next camp as per news by villagers. Hence, we were sure that the next trekking path will be muddy. Some more mountains were having snow due to snowfall. Coldness increased. A mist came down in valleys was impatient to reach upward. Steam was coming out while speaking. Sunrays entered and were pleased with the cool weather also. Everyone returned after their morning rites.

I was ready with 'My' Binocular. A beautiful Bird flew away, which was seen on the very first day at Base camp. He was driving to and fro for 2-3 hundred meters. He was carrying something in his beak while shifting from one tree and leaving that tree after some definite period. He was doing that frequently.

He might be building a nest. I was aware of how much one needs to travel for getting a home. Others observed us watching something with a binocular and he was focused in limelight from sunlight. We saw 3 more birds in the same direction. Many photographers set a camera towards them. Everyone was eager to capture its picture and waiting for one glimpse of the bird hidden in the greenery. You will be important if you appear rarely.

We started wandering in a village looking at multi-colored birds having different behavior. Since a day before some were sitting frequently alone at one place. Some were with his partner. Most of the Habits of birds were found similar to human beings. Sorry, I think human being has stoles some habits from birds. Leaving a home early morning for work, returning home after work, building a home, keeping babies in other's nest, getting wet in the first rain and many habits are copied from birds. But luckily he could not fly and it saved the place for nests. Otherwise, the sky would get divided like earth. Like plots in Square feet, the atmosphere in cubic feet would have also sold.

We came to the village at the cricket ground. We had to charge our batteries on camera and mobile too. Someone gave Rs. 10/- to shopkeeper near the ground for the same need. I requested at one home. You can name it as over-advantage or greediness we arranged three plugs connection. A lady in that home prepared a bed for us. It was looking like sewed at her home only. We asked her for tea for five moody men, she went to the kitchen immediately. We sat quietly. She came with a tea and we looked at each other and made a gesture of appreciation only having very first sip. She did not know Hindi, so we could not communicate with her. We will remember that tea made up of cow milk and lemongrass. After having the tea, we got more energized and roamed forward. We reached the school where there was a single room for two standards. Maybe, the classroom was not opened for many days when we saw inside of the room through the broken bars of a window. It was there to show the example of an airless and unclean room. Comparing the room, it was a clean and more beautiful place everywhere outside the room. There was not a place to sit even for teachers so we did not expect benched for students.

After looping to a school we reached the Cypress tree with the diameter biggest than all those trees seen before. To check its diameter we hugged that tree by keeping hands in hand by 6 people. Later, we came to know that it was a holy place for villagers.

Somebody's mobile was showing a network range and

everyone took out their mobile. There was full network coverage and everyone conveyed their well-being to home. We made one call to our colleague and everyone contributed part to make him jealous of our journey. We returned to our tents.

The President of one of the charitable foundations, residing in the village and working for the development of the village, was giving a speech. 10 young supporters were with him. He was not asking for any kind of donation, but he was only requesting to put up his opinion about facilities available and not available & how it can be available there through the developing medium of internet. Since we are from cities & from different states; the effect of raising awareness on such developmental issues will be faster & from different states. It will give an overall impact on the government and may pay attention here. He, his team were honest and having only this expectation.

I left the speech in the beginning and I joined back very late. Slowly, one after the other started looking here & there. Some movements started. Some of them were staring at him. By looking into their eyes & faces one can easily guess that they have lost their mind in a different world. A speech was betting longer & the movements of listeners also increased. Suddenly we saw a sign of darkness. But it was not the end of the day. A shower of rain washed the ground & all went to the respective tent. Very shortly, within 5 minutes all came out. Speakers & rain moved away together.

Everything was going slowly. There was no hurry at all. It was a great satisfaction of staying for a day at the right place. At base camp, the number of trekkers might be increasing by around 50 per day & the group ahead at higher height must be bearing a high coldness. We could imagine it on basis of our imagination. There was no network definitely. Vice FD reached our camp. We realized that we will be having only a concert today not cards.

Sun got tired and left for the day but we were still feeling enthusiastic. Everyone sat in the darkness. Mr. Khole & Natu Uncle started to sing. The show started with a Gazal & ended with a Lavani. A collection of good songs was about to end and we reached to current Good Songs. All old songs are not good and all-new songs are not bad. Everyone was sure that we will be moving to the next camp on the next day. It was not required to say "Good Night".

Jungle Book

"Good Morning", Sun wished & all awaken with enthusiasm. Before starting the trek, everyone repeated a prayer sung by Natu Uncle. For so pleasant and memorable two days, we thanked Mr. Khole Sir & started walking. He had to stay at that camp for the next 20 days.

We were heading in a direction shown by Khole sir, which was the same which was used by boys yesterday early morning. Most of them were saying that they would choose a spot at a longer place if the path would be known already. We named some of the points as Pankaj point, Vinayak Point to different locations.

A day before, those who were lagging behind in a group were walking far ahead today deliberately. It was an experience that they keep lagging behind continuously & those who go ahead far away at the front, get bored after waiting for followers for a longer period. These slow movers were getting tired and were blocking the rest of all others. Most of the trekkers wanted to continue their pace. In addition, it was difficult to stand in a very narrow path & slippery valley. Unless the people ahead don't move further all had to halt. Broken trunks of Cypress trees were creating more hurdles in a path. Now, everyone had recognized other's faces so everyone was taking help from anyone. To push someone for his progress, to keep yourself behind for the same sake are the qualities given by

Trek which improves your behavior as a human being. Many times we were checking the path before the whole batch decides to move further.

When we were moving ahead, we were guiding others on how to keep foot or ankle exactly & for how much time a leg should be kept behind. A slope was high enough that we were also taking support of roots of trees after digging for proper grip. Each tree whether it is alive or broken, burned or dried, it's all parts were helping us.

After some time, it was difficult to find the path because most of the ground was covered by mulch. We were checking whether it was soil or rock below our feet. It was required to move towards the right or to the left with a small angle to reach the place at looking at a high angle. Nair Uncle, age about 60 Years, was resting again & again. Those who were bigger in size, weight, or age were having more frequency of having a rest. Unknowingly, we- I, Vinayak & Vasant Rao from the Bengaluru group had a responsibility to be with them. Anushri offered a Glucose powder & when I was accepting it by the hand she suggested quickly eating it that directly by mouth as my hands were not clean. Those were so careful words. Pavitra, Nair Uncle, Anushri, Jitendra, Meghana, Suman, Abhiram, Abhijeet; a team came together and now we were part of their team. We were helping some of them to reduce the weight of their bags by eating some of the items!!

Space we were getting rarely to stand was not enough for a single person. Because of placing foot on a rock continuously by one after or because of someone's weight, stones were getting loos from soil and then falling in the valley. We were thankful for the weather since it was not raining there. It was difficult to imagine how much muddy this way could be in rain.

Those who were having a halt to see us, we were sitting beside them. It was the same time when they start to move ahead due to a long boring halt. Again, those who were at the front in a queue early morning started lagging behind the group later. I was one of them. We were getting responses after shouting loudly so many times to know the direction. We were checking all possible ways except the way to return. We were not having answered whether to stop just because we were lagging behind or to have a rest. The direction of a shout by Vinayak was not the direction of the walk. Even if we could found the way, we were not sure that it will help trace the direction of response. Cypress trees all around were looking the same. Everyone with me was confused and lost. Still, we were shouting one after one in a different language. We heard a loud voice. And we realize that we will be having some surprises ahead. We started walking again. A shouting got lowered because those friends might have moved forward & suddenly myself & Rakes shouted at the same time.

We were looking to the ice near our feet at the ground. At first, I was having doubts about whether it is ice or only fungus. It was the same doubt like a bag in a local train is empty or it contains a bomb. We did not hesitate to touch the substance looking like a fungus, in that dirty getup. Appearance like not having a bath for so many years, after crawling wherever possible and after touching anywhere to different surfaces in the whole day, it was not easy to touch fungus. However, for a moment I touched it carefully. It was the first snowball lying on the ground. We dig out that hard ice & cleaned our hands. On the way ahead there was some snow on both sides. We recharged and started walking ahead, throwing big balls of snow far away. It was a flat road but having turns.

Padri, 9300 Feet.

Four to five tents were waiting for us. A giant vertically mountain behind that Tent was appearing as if it is for our security only. Chilled water was jumping from the top of a rock on the right side. We could not imagine its temperature since we did not experience it yet. Water, flowing from the cascade was very near to the tent. An Icy mountain appearing from Base Camp was so closer and bigger from here. We had to turn our chin up to see the top of the mountain. Mr. Khole told that the camp leader will expect more discipline than him. But we were pleased to see "Mohd Rafi", Shirish. I hugged him by calling Rafi Sahab. He welcomed everyone.

Our tent was just beside the cooking tent. As usual, it was booked by Amol, by keeping the bag very first, inside the tent. Throwing a bag inside, and keeping those wet gloves on the tent to dry I ran to the hearth in the cooking tent. I was looking for a fire after so many days. As I was doing a handshake with fire after playing with Ice stone, I heard a whistle for me. It was not permitted to go inside this cooking tent. I left the tent immediately. Everyone forgot how many kilometers of the distance they have ascended. Mukesh & I started doing one dance step. Anyone, anywhere, in any position, could do this move & we both were doing this step in the office, sitting facing & bearing each other daily and got approval to leaves from the same boss. Today we were dancing on the correct platform.

Horses were having their dinner at moorland near to our tents. I was about to fall on the face when I was running behind them alacrity & ardently. I failed to capture a photo of a running horse as he ran away. I returned hiding a small defeat. Actually, legs were also painting so much, but our stubborn mind did not allow for a rest. Shirish announced the practice of walking over ice. That area was near about 5-10 minutes walking distance. As he called without a whistle we moved quickly. It was raining slightly, so we carried a plastic cover with us.

Once again, we started gossips how 5 minutes becomes 25-30 minutes. Out of 45, only 25 friends were with us. We were going through the way in a dense forest. It was difficult to know where to go exactly? Suddenly soil disappeared and we were started slipping since our feet were over ice only. There was a hillock covered entirely with snow. No soil, no Stones, no mud, no leaves. Do they even exist?

Beautiful clean ice till far distance & I kept very first step on Ice. Slightly slippery, making a careful move for a second step. Till that time first step has made an impression. Slipping or walking again & again. Anyone whose support was being taken, he was slipping too.

Everyone was placing baby steps after so many years. It was difficult to balance over a slope. It was no painting but it was fun to fall down. Shirish informed us about a tree of Birch after removing the bark of one tree. This is a rare tree & can be seen in the Himalayas only. In the early centuries, Kings that time were using it as paper to write, Shirish informed. One small piece was enough as a memory of Himalaya but since it was available & it may vanish anytime due to transition by human any time, I removed longer barks & put it in a bag of binocular.

At some distance, many of us were enjoying slides like a child & shouting continuously. Climbed up on a hillock, you can say, a heap of ice' of about 15 to 20 meters in height. Kept my legs straight downwards, pushed slightly & and started slipping downwards very funnily. We enjoyed those slides a lot and shouted aloud with slight fear too. It made us forget tiredness and boosted us to walk for a further 10 km in just 20 minutes. I remembered slides at a water resort at a family picnic. My younger cousins could have more fun here. With their memories, I climbed up that heap of ice again. Vishal & Mukesh seated on a plastic raincoat were calling me. They were making me hurry up as they were about to sleep at any moment and wanted to slide together for more fun. As I seated on plastic, all three slipped. Started together but turned in three different directions. I reached the bottom of the slope with my head downwards. We were just laughing continuously without standing up. We were telling this incident to those who had already seen this & we were also telling each other!! They were listening too!!! It was full of unexpected in the trek. I did not see such photos on the website of YHAI and did not remember such a photo was shown by my colleagues who came here one year back.

We had to reach our camp before dark. I removed more bark of birch & put it in a bag as I may not meet that tree again. Returned to the forest and started finding their ways.

Myself, Mukesh & Vishal; were walking lazily & very last in the group with a big gap. Shirish didn't know that we were stopped behind to pee. It started raining heavily. I had taken a plastic raincoat cover overhead which was only allowing the sound of raindrops. Shirish a camp leader was waiting at some distance shouted for not giving any response when he was calling us repeatedly. He gave us a long lecture, but after listening to our true reason & since we couldn't hear through the plastic cover he became calm.

Shirish informed about the existence of bears in that area. "If beer is pursuing you, what will be your action?" Shirish asked. Only & the last solution for us was to run, of course. He replied to run downwards. While running downwards his hair disturbs him & his running speed retards, he explained.

It was darkened when we reached the tent. We had a queue in a short time for dinner. Coldness of water was not bearable, experienced while cleaning our hands before dinner while splashing on the face, drinking the water with a cup of palms at a stream. So we were sharing plates with two or three friends to avoid cleaning more plates. Each chapati was getting finished as soon as it was being picked. That plate was being filled so many times by everyone, but there was no discipline at all to finish that food. Like everywhere we had a buffet but someone has to put lights by keeping the torch towards the plate. A plate had only a touch of that chilled water and was not cleaned properly. We were behaving boorishly.

A hill covered with snow was luminous in dark too. It was actually looking like one of the shiny stars because of light from a moon. Some of the portions over stone & trees were appearing as black marks on the moon. The continuous sound of cascade….dark blue sky…. twinkling stars……five tents under the security of a mountain….cold water flowing near a tent….. The atmosphere was pleasant…….and a spirit of Mohd Rafi entered Shirish & we were chorus for him. There were 30 to 40 listeners at the beginning. Slowly, that number reduced to 10 since some did not know Hindi & some were wanted to sleep. Some of them realize that we are not an audio cassette; we are an MP3 player, so that number reduced to 5-6. It's a tragedy if someone doesn't face any tragedy & this reflects in sad songs. Just because of the rule and sad response, a concert got abandoned by all singers.

It was a nice experience of sleeping in the sleeping bag the previous day. So, some of us had quarreled with Shirish, as the total no of the sleeping bag was less than several batch mates. Those who did not get a sleeping bag got two blankets each. I & Amol were ready to place one on the carpet & 3 to cover.

That night, I had taken initiative to tie the knots of the door to replace Amol as a precaution for midnight. I had a show at the new planetarium. I was less happy that time since there was no one to share the same scene. Happiness increases if you share it. I kept my body on the floor. Eyes covered themselves.

Ups, Downs and Ups

A new day rose with a new aim to reach a higher height. Sunset was at one corner & today sunrise from another corner. After forgetting the day, date, time now it is time to forget the names of directions. Up above to reach there, down sometimes; these were the only two directions that exist. A night was for a very short duration. Starting a day using chilled water is expected & a habit now. I increased the amount of water in a body by drinking hot tea in larger quantities. Everyone was in a queue with empty tiffin boxes after washing them and removing yesterday's leftovers early morning to carry the next packed lunch in Tiffin boxes.

Disciplined Shirish whistled & ordered to form a queue. Dr. Vijay, from Gujarat but speaks in Punjabi style. Everyone copied his style while shouting a sequence number in a queue. It was the symbol of enthusiasm that is directly proportional to elevation. Those, came with their respective groups were standing in a queue in initial days, were standing in any position in any queue beside anyone.

Journey started. The color of everyone's shoes became the same after descending a muddy slope in beginning. Once your clothes and shoes get dirty, you can sit or crawl anywhere. It was repetitive beauty of nature, sceneries & so the frequency of capturing a photo, viewing through binocular reduced. Only professional photographers or those who were carrying a costly camera were still framing the landscapes. I was feeling considerable weight loss. I was happier due to the reduced shape & lowered size of my stomach. Unchanged Pant since the first day was proof. You feel pleasure sometimes when you lose something.

I had tried to lower extra fats by regular exercise. I did not see a mirror for a longer time. People were identifying me as the only success; but because they were with me daily. I was sure about a change of my skin tone continuously but it was difficult to judge the exact darker shade & imagining my own face. I hate this guess.

We had crossed the Parvati River very frequently. At one point I jumped on ice hurriedly where water was flowing below it and after jumping. Placing a foot in the wrong spot could be dangerous. I had taken a stick as support. Ankles were paining due to cracks. A portion of the leg below the knees was bearing a weight of the whole body. In this situation also everyone was helping each other without any expectation. After breaking 3-4 sticks we realized how the stick should be with you. One was walking just because the person ahead was moving ahead & because the person behind him needs space to move ahead. Forget about the mimicry; I could not speak in my own voice too. The trekkers ahead were criticizing those who were lagging. Those were in the middle, having an opinion that, those that are ahead are in too hurry & those who are lagging are just wasting a time. The last group was suggesting enjoying the beauty of nature. Initial groups according to state, field, language, age changed to forward, middle & tail. I could see my other eight members during lunch or in the tent only. We did not capture any photos of my own group. So I was taking snaps of others and I was also being part of their memories.

The guide came back to search for us. Nair Uncle shouted at him. He could not get an opportunity to speak a single word. Because of Uncle, I found one more voice and style for mimicry. While listening to his continuous lecture was funny for me till we reach the open flat surface.

All had finished their lunch. We sat at an extreme edge of the ground at keeping our legs in the air. I opened a tiffin box from the bag & washed my Hands by rubbing them over my T-shirt & pants. We finished a lunch of Rotis & potatoes. Mukesh, Vishal, Vinayak helped Presida to reach this point. As she thanked us for this, we asked for 'Maggi' for us. We got a hot Maggi at this height & finished it fast as it was bought & brought by none. Do you know? Maggie can't be prepared in two minutes but can be finished in 2 minutes in two spoons by four persons in one dish.

All, including the guide, finished lunch & moved forward after rest where I want to have a permanent tent to stay for some days at a nice flat place. But as I moved up by doing rock climbing, an area in front of the ground was looking dangerous and at an almost right angle. Moving up between rocks was looking more difficult as everyone was standing frequently to get a place for any movement. Due to such an increase in breaks, we who were lagging were getting a needful rest. Though they were good at walking continuously I could reach them very easily by climbing utilizing the experience of 25 Forts. Even muscles were getting stretched in a new different & difficult angles were so useful.

The distance was decreasing between two who were

walking, sorry, jumping ahead. Whichever that distance was it was because of bags. Everyone was caring to keep a safe distance as the bag was hitting the follower. It was so narrow a path that one foot can be kept horizontally. On the left side, it was almost vertical slope till the ground. A stick in the right hand was giving support to the body & small plants on the mountain giving motivation.

Mukesh was ahead of me, Suman was ahead of Mukesh, then Abhiram then Vinayak. After crossing a hurdle of stone, Abhiram turned to give hand to Suman but he slipped fallen there. Suman shouted in a typical way as it can be heard in old Hindi movies. Even Vinayak also shouted in the same typical style. Abhiram was lucky, but later we harassed Vinayak, why he shouted for a boy? We did not give any importance to Abhiram's fall. But why being male, Vinayak shouted for Abhiram?

After walking for a longer distance, 5-6 villagers were found chit-chatting. From this point, we could see the previous lunch point, next camp, village 'Grahan' & way for the next camp. Instead of four directions, these were the four important things for us.

Those villagers informed us about poor weather and the difficulty to find a way ahead. For the same reason, the SP-1 group was sent back after waiting one additional night to check whether the weather is clearing off. "Everything will be fine", they motivated.

Anyway, there was an absence of teamwork noted in a program at base camp. We stayed for one extra day at Grahan, that time they faced heavy rain. They faced most of the negative things. We were with the right friends at right time here. Nature was happy with us & us too. You have to not only think positively but also act positively.

But why these villagers are here? They should be at the next camp carrying the material for the next tents? Whether tents are ready at the next camp or not?

It was new scenery like in Bollywood movies. A Green Mountain is having a cleanly seen narrow way. At the same slope, four tents appeared like they are placed at the edge of a hill, a single tree behind tents and a sky with a different color. By mistake a wrong color is selected by a brush for painting or the color has changed its shade after getting dried. For me it is difficult to describe coldness; as such equipment was not available to measure it in degree Celsius & I was not having such experience before.

Camp leader welcomed. After shaking hands with me, he continued waiting for someone. I proudly informed, "I am the last, forty-sixth". Tea-snacks were waiting for us. The camp leader approached for a snack & said to wait for the news. Mukesh questioned instantly, "News will be good or bad?" Discussions started in groups.

Ratapani, 11000 Feet.

I reduced the weight of my body parts by removing the jacket, sweater, and gloves. I was willing to change my clothes but my body was not ready for those movements. A pair of socks was no more because of suffocation in dirty shoes after using them for continuous 5-6 days. Another pair, relative of the first pair, had no idea of this mishap. I kept my Shoes at the backside of the tent so that they can be identified by looking at the pattern and thickness of mud over it. As tents were fewer, we were 14 trekkers in the same-sized tent.

Somewhere at a considerably longer distance, a rubber pipe was placed to make water available for use from melting ice. It consumed half an hour to reach that spot & 15-20 minutes to get a chance to wash hands, faces & tiffin. One after one, everyone was rubbing his face. We did not have any other option for cleaning and that's why we were using that chilled water. Did you ever splash water from the freezer? I wanted to have experience of this coldness wearing only a T-shirt & pants. We returned to the tent where the same villagers were sitting around an actual bonfire. At least I could wear a sweater & then return to the fire, but painting my legs & lazy mind did not permit me to move away. The shivering fire was barely sharing possible heat.

I asked villagers about the possibility of our next upward movement. I was unaware that the camp leader was near to them. He shouted at me for not wearing a sweater. I kept a mum did not move. He raised his voice & started telling list about problems that could happen in that cold atmosphere to anyone with such getup. I did not have any option other than to return to the tent.

It was a full dark. Don't know whose dish was that. By keeping a torch in hand and after walking downwards near the tent by raising the paining ankles with cracks I could search Mukesh, Amol, Vinayak & Vishal. It was difficult to identify whose hand from which way to share food on the plate. Fortunately, food was going before it gets cooled in his own mouth at least. We were worrying since a place for attending nature's call at night or early morning was far away. Because of this fear we may have less food. We wiped our hands with water. Passed the same amount of water through throat & then drunk a cup of hot Bournvita. After a 10 Km trek, 20m distance from dinner location toward tents was like another 11th Km for us.

14 people in a tent were ready to sleep closely. Sleeping Bags also had occupied their Uncle tired of searching his glove. He slept. We also searched a lot. I realized that I have also misplaced one glove. I was doubting Nair Uncle how he can sleep easily? I was bored finally and fell asleep. I slept wearing a newly known thermal wear. While sleeping we were sensing the slope of a mountain.

We can save the power of batteries by keeping them in pockets in the shirt or pants you wear. So I kept all ten batteries in my different pockets. I was sleeping in style by keeping one hand missing glove in my pocket. Moon was so closer at 2:30 p.m. It was not new to look at him at this time when he was looking at me and I was feeling ashamed.

A next day, with an unknown date, time, month, age, year, place. We don't know and don't want to know. We woke up too early at around 4:30 a.m. only for the next move. We were ready after usual ineffective morning rites.

Even for school, college or office also I did not get prepare so early. Comparing with school, college & office I was quicker in getting ready. What was there to prepare? I had already worn all my clothes last few days. Suddenly I found my gloves out of somewhere.

But a camp leader was passing bad news to different groups that our batch may not move ahead. Atmosphere changed. We, overexcited, decided not to return without the summit. Bengaluru group, we nine, most of the photographers, one who missed this opportunity last year too, was not listening at all. Those who found this trek difficult and reached here after a lot of hard work were not opposing the camp leader. It was surprising that the group leader, Mr. Rathore, himself & all of his tent-mates were ready to return. The batch was divided into two groups, one who was so eager to go high & another who was happy after reaching till here. Mr. Desai from Goa was holding our national flag of India 'Tiranga' & taking a snap with a group. Was it the destination where we were? Was it a victory? For me, it was shameful to stand beside Tiranga. So I avoided being a part of a photo.

Our group leader, Mr. Rathore said in Gujarati style, "As a group leader, I announce that we all are going back". I reacted immediately, "Is this your opinion or opinion of the whole group? We will not act as you told us; actually, you have to do what the group will decide. Have you communicated with a group? If you want to go alone, then you can. My raising voice made Mr. Rathore keep mum. Some more voices rose after me. The group leader who was not involved in any activity since the beginning was aside now. The aged uncle also got the same reply with disrespect.

A day before, when I was near a bonfire, I saw a villager demanded an extra amount for their service, I remembered. Some were doubting with the management of "Youth Hostel". The reason for bad weather was also not easily believable. Because there was no rain last two days & today atmosphere was so clean & clear. It was difficult to understand the exact reason. We did not have any option other than listening to a camp leader and that is the trekking manners when you are going with a big organization. Anyway, can u find the route alone? But we were protesting as possible as we can. Leaving the target in half is an insult of hard-worked by you for the achieved half? Voices were becoming louder to express the protest & frustration. It was like an argument on news channels.

Luckily none of the media reaches here because there are no controversies at all in the village. If they show the beauty of nature then it will become a tourist place and will affect peace. Some of us were capturing photos of this argument too. Even the dog was upset & sited, not showing his face to anyone. We can express ourselves in a variety of words, languages, gestures & postures but a calm dog was giving a hint that we have to follow him.

It was an unwanted return journey. I was striking the stick on trees & stones with little upset, which was used for support while going up. We were looking to the upset eyes of each other and consoling each other. For a fun, we were using the same dialogues which the camp leader used to console us. We were abusing those officemates who were wishing for bad luck as a part of jokes. Even I got bumped by one of the branches of a tree. We were in a direction to the village 'Grahan'. At least we could enjoy river rafting as we were reaching the base camp some days before. Plan of river rafting in an oscillating boat at Bias River was passed to everyone and most of them were looking ready. All stopped to one plane ground.

Villagers in a tent were ready with their shop. They were waiting for us only. How they came to know that we are about to reach there? The Vice field director Mr. Tiwari was ascending towards us. As he reached us, Vishal complained, we supported him.

"Nothing will happen; everything is fine, let's go". Mr. Tiwari said & we all were inspired with full energy. We had Hi-Fi with many. Again a journey started in a jungle upwards. The path which we were using for descending same as for ascending. It was laughing at us and now looking at our happy faces he must be feeling jealous.

The very first-time sweat was running over a body. Unknowingly we moved down a great height and while going up we needed longer steps. We were stopping frequently. In a short span, around half an hour, we had covered a long distance. Water bottles were empty. Some were reached at a far distance due to great enthusiasm. Some of our batchmates decided to return to Grahan Village. We could easily guess some names. It was a surprise that Mr. Natu, aged around 50-55 years was having great courage & Mr. Kamath, with the same age passing a joke continuously were ahead of us. Both of them were an inspiration that day. It took two hours to go up, from where we moved down in 45 minutes.

The same camp leader welcomed us. We returned very special thanks. A way to reach some thousand feet was opened already. We were not having a key only which was with Field Director. Now, that door was broken & we were about to enter from a door of success.

31 out of 46 moved to further heights. Nair Uncle & the group decided to return except Suman and Abhiram. Two doctors who came with Dr. Vijay from Gujarat & two old men were not sociably in a group from the first day. All from one tent, who had taken a photo with Tiranga with Mr. Desai and Group Leader Rathore returned to the 'Grahan'. It was not a right that I was feeling better than some trekkers are going back having negative thoughts, and we were also unhappy as we could not say goodbye to any of them. We never met again and neither taken their contact numbers and they are not my social media friends. We could do that on the very first day. I remember Jitendra forced me to stand on his leg to stand when there was a very slippery slope. He also left the journey. Kapil was promoted to a Group Leader. He was actually suitable for this position. But he instantly said that we all are leaders. This is one of the qualities of a leader.

Tiffin which was filled up at this camp made empty at the same place. After lunch & storing some chilled water in our stomachs, our next journey was about to begin. In all these processes, we wasted almost three hours and we could have easily utilized it to go far away to a more height. But whatever happened, I think, was the mental and physical test. It was not easy to reach this height. We passed an exam attended in last 3 hours.

All the necessary goods were not reached the next camp yet. Parts of tents, iron rods, thicker sleeping bags, were placed at the lower camp only. Everyone agreed to carry each bag which was an additional weight. We disdained to the weight of bag & carried it with us. Some of the lady villagers were ready to carry our main bag & sleeping bag with Rs. 150/- charges. Shreejith, among us, gave his bag to one lady. Of course, handling a camera was more important for him.

All moved away till I was packing my bag. Removing a binocular out, I packed my bag in a great hurry. Again I was the last person. I was angry with Amol, who helped Natu Uncle to pack his bag and only gave suggestions to me & further went with 4-5 friends in the front.

Started feeling tired after 20 to 25 steps. A camp leader was behind me. If he reaches then it was an indication that the entire batch has reached a particular spot. A bag on my back was having imbalance. I was searching for a stick on a narrow path. After breaking so many sticks I found a good stick. I smiled continuously when I did my shopping for this trek at Bhandup.

We reached the same stop from where four directions could be seen as a day before. Everyone tied their sleeping bag properly and then moved ahead. A group of SP-3 was having lunch on the ground where we were a day before. Both the group shouted to respond to each other.

A new way started. It was called as a way just because there was someone ahead of me and who was walking. A sleeping bag carried by us was tempting us to sleep anywhere. We tried to reduce the weight of water bottles by drinking them again & again. We were tired & re-tired after 20-25 steps. There was no tree at a long distance in any direction. Going down for an hour in beginning, then two hours for moving up & break for one hour, a total of 4 hours forced us to now walk under the hot sun. The very first time, we were experiencing the high intensity of sunlight. We could realize the effectiveness of goggles after removing them same.

We could see some villagers were ascending from a far distance towards us. Their age was double that of ours and were carrying the weight triple than that we were carrying. The length of the metal pillars was about 6 to 6.5 Feet. Half of the length of the three pillars was on the back and the remaining half was above the head. Carrying the tools and equipment they reached us very fast. We were having a halt frequently but they were walking continuously. We looked at them with amazement when we gave them space to walk. Even some ladies carrying luggage crossed us and moved a far distance ahead of us. Villagers were used to this but a porter in cities also may not lift this much weight. Handling quarrels with them would be a different issue. Before 'Garibrath Express' reaches Bandra Station, porters were having a similar argument. All these movements were happening only for our tents.

There was a slope entirely covered with snow so we

could walk at the edge of the hill. There was no support on both sides. We could walk by force only with the support of a wooden stick we were looking closely to the spots covered with snow instead of a clear path of soil. Early morning, we could start ascending here in speed; but walking down for 3 hours had made it difficult to climb again with the additional weight of bags. One was placing his second foot just to relax the first foot. Then third, then fourth, and so on. We were continuing pouring water in our stomach as fuel in the fuel tanks of automobiles. By putting foot once in snow and then in the soil there was more than enough mud on both the shoes to feel the heaviness. I was blaming that weight of mud also for reducing my speed. Even socks became wet after shoes exhausted their capacity to carry ice water.

Finally, we could see rush at the corner of one hillock. On a flat surface over a mountain, someone had set up a snack corner by tying a plastic sheet over four bamboos. We were looking for some food passionately. Some moved forward after having tea or Maggie noodles or both. We also kept our bags wearily. I had never imagined that I will have tea leaving my legs loose in a valley. Weird wishes were coming true. After having Maggie also lifted our bags and ready for the next challenge. Who works harder than at the office after getting leaves?

Support by stick was more reliable than own legs. It was difficult to step ahead without setting a stick in the snow. Some were getting suggestions to leave someone's hand and be independent while walking. A habit of getting help makes you weaker and the person who helps is also responsible for the same. I was thinking mathematically, at least one among 31 trekkers may lose his balance. Whole-body was painting. Sometimes we're getting bored to search the way and the place for afoot. We could rarely find a reliable stone, in wet soil from where snow was melted, to put afoot. Training for soldiers rather than experience at the battlefield which is shown in movies or we read in articles was similar to this. Soldier mentioned in the Novel 'Mahanayak' which I was reading were struggling to reach India from Myanmar in the same manner. There is no obvious comparison with them. We did not hit by the bullet and no one was injured at all.

However, we could trust our physical capabilities to become soldiers. An upward slope with zig-zags was not ending and my friends at the top started capturing photos with smiles who were reaching to the top of the slope having only snow. It was a beautiful spot to camp.

It's a Victory

Nagaru: 12400 Feet.

Villagers cleaned that area in such a way that it was looking there was no snowfall at all. Looking at the thickness of ice around one imagine the efforts behind removing that hard ice. There were only two tents for gents & a Separate tent for 4 girls aside. A separate small tent was made for canteen staff and workers which were not looking strong. They had just completed their work. There was a flat portion of 10-12 Feet behind our tent. Looking down from that border, a slope of the mountain was appearing like a length of a finger. It took 2 to 2.5 hours to reach this top. The path which we used was not at all visible. Everyone was enjoying their being at this place. Everyone was having handshakes, hugging everyone. Himalaya at all four sides. Himalaya, means Aalaya of Him, house of Snow.

'My dear Sun' was ready for Sunset. At the backside, there were tents and a cold carpet of ice. On a left, there was a way to reach the topmost point which was not visible till now. On the left side, there is only a giant mountain & in front of me another mountain occupying perfect space covering my complete vision through both eyes. This mountain was too big as it was the endpoint of earth. Greenery over the mountain was looking like Henna on a palm. On a right, there was one more mountain looking like an ice cream coming out of the cone. The wave of ice stopped at the edge with fear of the valley where I was looking to the view. There were only mountains of Ice wherever my sight could reach.

You must have read in Geography that Himalaya was formed by big waves of the ocean only. Its height is higher when you measure it concerning sea level. Therefore it was difficult to forget the bottomless sea. Sea only has formed Himalaya so Himalaya should return all melted water through rivers as a gesture of gratitude.

Himalaya is also doing great work by storing water in form of ice. Actual pollution was started when humans started having a bath in the Holy Ganga River. He started complaining when it started affecting only human's health while drinking & bathing. He started finding different reasons. So, it's a better idea to store Water which will get dirty till it reaches the sea, will become salty & in summer when there will be a shortage of water after melting the ice. This is an It's a much better way to store the water in dams by forcing farmers to sell their land & spending so many millions.

To praise this work, the shower of small cool flowers started over the Himalayas with some rain too. As I saw everyone was doing a call to someone I went to Vinayak. Amol was also having a chat on mobile. The full network was available. We are thankful to 'Airtel' – the network provider. I made a call to the first person & first friend of my life. I was badly missing her here. Instead of 'Hello', I said, "12,400 Feet". I said, "This a very beautiful place." While talking to her Himalaya was below my feet & Sun was also going down and I started crying. Frozen tears started melting. Voice gets lowered and no word could have heard on the other side. I can gift Himalaya, Sun, Moon, Sea & Sky, all these to that person, My Mother. As she asked, "Have you fallen anywhere?" I could not control my tears. Vinayak took a mobile loosely held in my right hand. He conveyed to my mom that I was fine & not injured. Vishal & Mukesh started kicking their legs to buttocks. Vinayak joined them later. I was crying while bearing this love and started remembering my father & brother who never hit me like this. Slowly everyone recall came in front of my eyes.

My home, school, college, relatives, office, company, neighbors; friends since childhood, college friends; trekking group, drama group; a dog kept for two days, a parrot left a cage who could not speak; my bike, cricket, music, paintings, oratory prizes, all the legends about whom I read in a book; all the visited places, forts, everything. My life is nothing without all of them. Everyone put colors in my life same as the colors I could see in the scenery everywhere around me. I couldn't do anything other than dropping a tear. It feels bad and sad if you have done nothing for others. I stopped crying.

Here, Sun started his performance. I came closer to the boundary. While dancing during a snowfall, my belt tied to the waist was so loose already. I came forward for two steps to look at the sun &.........alas!

He was my friend which was carried like Kangaroo. A witness of so many happy moments, my camera, fell on the ground and had one bounce before disappearing at the boundary of the mountain. I was about to get it, but it bounced over slop and moved further & further. I was looking at him till it reaches the edge & disappeared. I was silent and motionless. I could not react. There was no one. Those who saw this incident from a longer distance asked me "It was only cover, right?" I denied.

True Breaking News got spread everywhere & most of them shown condolence. As suggested by someone I ran to Sherpa's tent & gave him details. I just pointed in the direction. Immediately he ran easily on slippery ice as an athlete runs in a race & even he could stop easily at the edge. His running surprised the spectators. For those who could not see how my camera rolled down over a slope, my camera allowed seeing that stunt. One more Sherpa ran away. Both returned quickly.

My mind had already accepted the fact. I tried to show

that nothing big has happened. I was upset deep inside but I had to enjoy in presence. The photo session was going on in the surrounding. I wanted fresh clothes on this occasion. I wore a short shirt removing the T-shirt. I decided to wear a pant, bought specially for this trek. It was surprisingly loose to my waist & even its chain was not proper. It was definitely not wearable. My friends could get an opportunity to get wacky photos & they will tease me later in the office. I carried the same pant which I was wearing for the last 10 days continuously. As I was tying the belt to the waist easily hand moved to the same position as the camera & .....I remembered the moment of losing my camera.

Snowfall continued. I was having tea waving both the legs towards the valley, but I could not seat there for a longer time. Nature started showing its game. As we were in a sky at some more height there was one more sky covered with black clouds. Looking like a running dark shadow of the mountain. Those clouds were at a speed which we were felling to the ground. It was just like an attack by them. Sun was going down behind so many mountains at a time finding the path between black clouds. Sunrays were trying to reach the mountain penetrating the cloud wherever possible. Sunrays were looking like rain only from some clouds. As the sun started going down sunlight behind one mountain got divided into two completely different colors. We, sorry my friends captured that scene.

This scenery can be described in a fictional way, but purposely described in simple words to let the reader imagine the exact picture. The colors and its shade were changing. Is it a new concept for painters? Eyes pleased as they were looking so many shades of different color at one time. Sunset was different at each moment. Sunset seen and captured at different locations till today were not so beautiful, I declared. It was one shade when I was looking with naked eyes, different when the camera bets placed near eyes & third after removing the camera. You need not do any setting for colors in-camera. People may doubt that these pictures are modified in Photoshop and may think all the real photos are also modified. I kept aside my friend's camera & was seeing the scene alone. Drama Ended.

With a loud whistling loudly camp leader alerted everyone & told them to go inside the tent. A blow of the wind became a storm suddenly. A cover of Sherpa's tent was about to fly away and one pillar was tilted. We received orders to hold our tents tightly. Priority was to prevent the air from going inside the tent. After everyone gathers inside, knots of cotton door tied very tightly to the middle pillar from top to bottom by Amol, the specialist. The direction of the wind was changing continuously. We kept all our bags at bottom of the cloth as weight. 2 Mates were holding one pillar, one at the top and another at the bottom. One was holding a center pillar at the top. Others slept at the border of a tent wherever they got space between bags. Although we were 14, we could see a large space inside. That storm showed that 10 more persons can easily stay in the same tent. We interchanged our positions for better grips. But the tent was still moving, rather swinging. As the force of wind increased we thought we all will go to go down in a valley. Everyone remained quiet after suggesting so many ideas for 20 to 30 minutes. Vishal pointed that someone was filling his own bag & many of us laughed. Some were laughed at deliberately & some did not laugh at all.

Sherpa, 17-18 years ago, came in a tent from the bottom of the tent. For a change, some of us started chatting with him in the same position. He left a school & started doing some work with various organizations. There were so many local boys doing a similar job. Some were asking very stupid questions to him. I remember someone asked him that are they eat rats as food? They were asking him the question about their lifestyle like they are in an exam hall and answering the last question related to their lifestyle!!

We could only smile looking at each other. He was the same guy who removed that plug from the switchboard without asking at base camp. We were in the same position for 10 minutes after Sherpa entered a tent. I got bored of holding tents. Even that storm did show something unexpected which is actually expected by him. All tents were safe. We heard a whistle for permission to come out. It was darker than earlier and was dinner time. Everyone had dinner very fast; within 10-15 minutes in a very small place. Hands got shake by that hot food. Filled the hot water bottle given by Sherpa by melting ice fallen near the tent. Oh! Water can become hot also! Just imagine you are having dinner at 12,400 feet. This reality itself was more enjoyable than any sort of a party. Stars were hidden by black clouds. It was complete darkness. There was no meaning at all to stand outside the tent. All went inside. It's safer being inside.

It was a proper decision to defecate on the same night than going early morning on the next day. Keeping torch & stick in hand we started walking on the slope of ice. Dr. Vijay & Natu's uncle was with me. The use of that torch was to find the path, but it was to avoid the border of a mountain. We selected a plot as away from tents as possible as we can. This time we could see our tents while sitting. Inserted a torch in ice, stick inserted inclined in ice on a slope to have strong support. Half of the pressure was used to hold the stick. Task completed. We washed our hands with hot water after so many days. Remember, you should book your name for earlier batches of the trekking. Else you will experience dirty surroundings later.

Quickly we went inside the tent. Amol, Vinayak, Vishal & Mukesh came inside, & were telling proudly that they had completed the task by holding hands with each other. It was crowded while we were sleeping in a tent that day.

This day was full of drama. Awaking earlier energetically, quarrel with camp leader & group leader, going down with the thought of failure, ascending again to the top, starting the next trek with the extra weight of the sleeping bag, losing a camera in a valley & a sunset which helped to forget all tiredness. We kept our self in a sleeping bag brought by us. The mind was still enjoying outside only. I had condolence to my dearest Camera.

At around, 1:30 a.m. I awake as usual. We were instructed not to go alone anywhere. That day Vishal also witnessed Stars that midnight in the planetarium. Ice on the mountain was looking bluish similar to the sky.

We heard the next whistle at around 3 to 3:30 a.m. Today we were moving to reach the topmost target. Nobody needed to get a refresh as already everyone was eagerly waiting for this morning only. Whichever bare minimum rest is required for the human body was already given. We had a warship with Sherpas at Nagaru. According to Sherpa, this is the place of Lord Naag. Everyone carried hot water in a bottle. I poured two cups of tea into my own stomach. Weight on the back was lowered as we served all the next batches by bringing the sleeping bags to this camp.

The journey started with multiple times of enthusiasm & pleasure. Today we had to walk entirely on ice & ice only. Walking without a stick was risky. Though we have stuck in hand there were chances of falling on our own face after slipping once you stand on toes for a moment while walking. Therefore, hand gloves became wet & it was again a punishment to carry ice in hands. I was fourth or fifth in the queue & looking at Sherpa who was creating a flat place for the first person for his step. The gap between the two trekkers was because of the bag only. Sherpas were encouraging everyone and shouting continuously. There was slight grass at the right edge. It was risky to put a step on the stone. On a left, there was such a slope that can send a person to find my camera in the depth of the mountain. Only Sherpa could stand easily and observing each & every one. They were moving speedily to help anyone in a queue.

We were moving our feet after 2-2 seconds. Suddenly the storm started as a few hours before. But this time we were not in a tent. We stopped on the spot. The storm stopped after 5-10 minutes. Without waiting for an order we started moving ahead. Storm gave us a hint to be alert & remained quiet. The wind was still moving madly. Everyone was concentrating on his own step. High Alert.

Just started again. Snowfall started. But this time everyone was familiar with a storm. Nobody was giving importance to the storm. Actually, everyone was enjoying snowfall again. We had to return to the camp if the weather would remain like this, the Camp leader announced. The decision of going back was more dangerous than falling from the top. Luckily snowfall & storm stopped. Most of us out of 31 were getting tilted like there is a pothole. Target was so close. We proved the song sung at the base camp. Vice F.D. Tiwari congratulated everyone.

13,800 Feet….. SUMMIT.

I felt satisfied that I have done something in my life. Marks obtained after studying for so many months & monthly salary after doing work for a whole month had so small importance than the feeling of success after reaching here. Marks and salary never created our identity nor given the satisfaction of something special had been done by you. In fact, whatever you get was getting compared with others & people surrounding you make negative comments frequently. Even I was also thinking negatively. But now I realized the true meaning of success, the height of success exactly after coming to this summit point. All faces were happy and proud. As all my friends reached the top we shouted, "Shivaji Maharaj Ki Jay!" We had a victory over natural calamities and our own limits.

A Lovely Fear

Everybody put Frooti which was kept in a bag while leaving Nagaru camp & celebrated this moment. Actually, no one could get the place to take it out while ascending and no one even could think about any item other than water. We were eating dry fruits like grams & grand nuts. From here onwards there was a big ground of ice. I was treating my Stick like a band and playing some strokes. Waving my stick here & there it was time to enjoy walking. After so many intervals everyone started chatting with each other. We never got an opportunity to walk along with anyone. Here 10 trekkers were walking together. Even I started speaking newly with my friends. But we could do this for a very small time. Everyone started walking in a queue by looking at a queue far away. We had a loop to the mountain of ice. We were walking like an ant having a heavyweight on the back continuously and only placing a foot on a stamp made by everyone who went ahead.

My feet were going deep, sometimes up to the knee. A friend behind me was giving me hand while I was helping a friend ahead of me. We write our name on a sea-shore & waves erase it. Here, we were writing names on waves themselves. We were walking on the sea of ice, giving autographs on a wave and moving ahead. That was not getting erased in front of our eyes. Instead of the wave goes away at the sea-shore we were going away from the waves. We tried to look around without goggle, but the intensity of reflection over snow was high and giving trouble. We were neither ascending nor descending. Our path was cutting the slope. Legs were going deep inside after two-four steps and we were spending more time for a smaller distance.

After half an hour it looked like the biggest challenge, a mountain-like wall of solid ice. My stick was already broken into 2 pieces. Sherpa threw it. I got angry like a child and took another stick thrown by someone. I found it after a lot of searches and it became my favorite while playing with that stick & used for writing on ice. After all, she was the only one who came with me keeping my hand in her hand. What would be that feeling if someone special comes with you for such a trek?

Inserting a new stick on a wall I started climbing. I did not have enough energy to bear the pain on my toes and knees but still, I was climbing a step one after one by putting in maximum effort. A stamp made by someone's foot could be called a step here; it was so brittle after most of the trekkers climbed up. Out of 31, I was second last. I didn't know when this has happened. Kapil was behind me & far away. It encourages you when someone is behind you. I put the stick near my waist. While taking the support of ice step that cold mountain was 5cm away from eyes. Sometimes a step was getting removed in hand when I tried to get support from it. Hand gloves were wet already but still were carrying out their responsibility very well.

After climbing 5-6 steps, we were standing to take a rest on the wall. It happened 10-12 times. After putting maximum energy to pull you, it again risked standing for breathing only for even 2-3 seconds. If that crushed slip away then I will not roll down, I will bump on the ground of snow. After huge efforts, a wall was climbed up successfully & it was again new a surprise ahead!!! I got a place to seat on a horse. One leg was towards one slope of mountain & another leg was at another. The height of the slope was near 100 meters. I was encouraging Kapil with a maximum loud voice from the mountain where I sat. Some were walking on the top edge & on the left side near about 250 meters, some mates were waiting for us. We started walking together; but how the gap increased?

It was again a fun time to slide over this bigger slope. Before that, it was a circus to walk on the top edge of a mountain without any support to both sides. No place to put a stick even. If you lose your balance you will lose your heart and then your body. You can do last help to everyone by making your body fall on the same side where your friends have reached. I put my feet on the same side and started walking with balance by keeping the brittle top boundary of the mountain to the right hand. Everyone was like a statue preparing him mentally, listening and observing instructions to a predecessor by Sherpa, waiting for their turn for a ride. After sliding from 250meters, everyone slipped 100 m away from the mountain. An artist sketched Ganesh at Base camp slept in different ways & went from different turns. He passed close to the stones and luckily not hit by rocks. Some were not following correct techniques and losing their direction. They were again laughing after finishing their slide. Some were capturing our photos from the bottom.

It was my turn; even I could not stand easily on a slope. I slept twice on a top but I leaned on one knee. One Sherpa kept his foot to keep me in that position. He made a flat place to sit. I sat comfortably. Keeping my legs straight and bag below my neck touched my back to the ground. Within that short time, I was inside a little bit on the ice. I pushed my body a little and Journey started. It was such a pleasant experience that made fear ran away. Without having efforts I was covering long-distance & I liked this new way. After a long time, hands & legs had a complete rest ….for full Two minutes.

Pant became wet while slipping. A shirt-in came out & ice got a space in a pant. I didn't want to stand on both legs actually. I was abusing that mad monkey who started walking on two legs. Why I am not a snake or earthworm?

No one other than human has reached here. We recalled that we saw a back of a kite through binocular when it was flying at a high height. At a considerable height, I heard a cawing sound. I praise that Crow & a dog came with us. He did not climb the wall. Sherpa lifted him on his shoulders and had a slide.

If I would not be a human being I could not have reach here. Though I would reach here, I could not survive here easily. First, I salute that person who found the clothes suitable for this weather. We wear jackets or shoes made by removing animal's skin. We use the hairs of animals for making clothes. We steal and use the efforts done by silkworms. A human being should be thankful to all the animals who give away their body parts & farmers who farm cotton. They are helping human beings to protect their body.

That slide forced Tiredness to run away. Kapil had a slide and brought some kilograms of ice. The same slope which was difficult to many with sleeping position, a Sherpa did skiing there without any equipment. We were watching him with wonder & he informed us that we will be going to this frequently ahead. The wonder of his slipping & opportunity ahead glided together over our faces.

After walking for 10 minutes only, we had to slide for a smaller depth & a less distance; but we had to ensure whether we have reached to right end. Again I positioned myself & gave a small jerk to my body & continued slipping. I was waiting for a stop, but suddenly I saw a slope double-deep and I was flying at double speed. The slope was so unexpected that I had fear for some seconds & huge enjoyment. Now it was difficult to judge the distance or depth I covered. Looking back towards the same direction it could spend 2 to 2.5 hours to climb, from where we have come down in 15 minutes. While looking to the wall from the opposite side now still neck had to tilt up. Everyone was in his own good mood, sharing his joy freely with everyone.

Sherpa captured a photo of 31 Trekkers who reached till here together. Someone clicked a photo for a group of nine. This photo will be memorable for everyone on that trek. Beside that location, there was a frozen lake. In the local language, Lake means 'SAR' and since we pass to the lake, it is named as SAR PASS trek. I recalled one of the lectures given at base camp.

Then everyone started experiments to slide together. We had an experience of plastic that if we put it below, the speed increases & the slide continues for a longer time. I put out plastic immediately from my bag. Plastic helped me for smaller slopes also, but again unexpected slope with one turn turns & turns started and ended. Now it was difficult to decide where I was going actually. No one was coming behind from the same slide. Away ahead was having immediate turn so no one was appearing. But now I could learn how to move ahead on the slope having turned, how to use a stick to avoid hitting trees standing in a path, how to avoid soil and rocks in between. I was using all the possible techniques at the right time. I was using that stick effectively. Sherpa waved his hands and I put breaks by inserting toes when speed was to be reduced. The mind was not ready for that break. I started walking in a direction shown by Sherpa.

Pant was completely wet already. But still, I was feeling cold somewhere to skin. Immediately I removed ice which entered inside the pant very fast before girls reach here. Suddenly a muddy way started & slipped on the spot too. Again & again after crossing the muddy ground & ice, I got bored. Even there was mud to socks. There was a new brown design on black pants too. While crossing one small stream I lose my balance and slipped on my buttock for the last time and reached to the tent shortly.

Many of us were resting in a tent. Many were waiting for the remaining all others. Some were still having sacks on their back, which might have reached recently.

I reached fourth from last. As all reached, everyone shouted, "Hip Hip Hurrah"

Biskeri Camp, 11,000 Feet.

'Rest' is best

As usual, Amol & friends reserved a separate Tent for the entire group. I threw my bag. Kept my shoes and socks on top of the Tent to make my feet free and allowed me to breathe everybody. Kept my all wet clothes to dry on the dry greenery. That was the only wearable pant that I had to leave on the ground. Size of the stomach was considerably reduced & satisfaction of this could be understood by those who have succeeded in reducing the same. I had to adjust pants given by Amol. While putting on the clothes in sunlight it was pure & ample. I was about to come into the tent to rest & suddenly rain started. So I ran here and there to collect clothes from my friends too. Collected all the clothes & thrown them in a tent. I really needed rest.

Very soon, I heard a whistle for snacks & tea. I recalled that I have not taken food since morning and did not feel hungry also. We ran to the tent for snacks. Mind was in greater speed than legs. We had hot onion Pakodas and tea having gossips like at office with friends. My friends left the kitchen. Later, the rain started heavily. I was not willing to make my clothes wet again. For some period, I was still ready to bear standing on my legs. But the rain was continuous. Snowfall also started. I had extra tea & snacks within that time. I was feeling jealous that all are resting inside & I was standing alone. Holding my slippers tightly between fingers I reached to the tent with slipping little. As

I was entering the tent, the rain stopped. Everyone was already passing comments & joking.

I was about to lie down I heard a whistle to take blankets to sleep. Now I was not at all ready to move for blankets. I could sleep without blankets also. Everyone waited for someone other will bring the same. Rakes went outside after deal of bringing blankets for Vishal with a condition that he will give his earphones to Vishal. Amol brought some no of blankets in a tent.

Putting two blankets on a body I allowed all body parts to rest.

Chinks on a toe were converted in chasms of an earthquake. A soil in chinks had to be tested to find to which village it belongs too. Legs were in an exact original position in a proper direction after using as a break on different rocks, mud, leaves in soil, in ice, on the ice wall, while putting break during snow riding. After competition with a stick, a portion of the leg from below the knee to toe became like a stick. If we walk without shoes for such a distance for continuous days our feet would get worn from the bottom! After slipping on ice continuously a portion from waist to the knees lost their sense of touch. I could take as many injections at this time & I was also ready to have a tattoo there. The flat portion after the biggest slide was not actually smooth. It was having speed breakers & many potholes that made a backbone feel the jerk. Comparing with knees, the fingers of the hand also did a great job. All fingers had suffered a lot while digging out roots of a tree to hold them properly, to dig hard ice & to have a support of same, to wash dishes, face; while drinking. After removing the bag also it feels like those belts are still over your shoulders. The neck was not moving properly by either looking down for a period or looking up continuously. An exercise of looking left-right while crossing the roads or checking the train time at one side & waiting for a train anxiously was not done for a longer time.

I had not seen my face for a longer time. So I am unable to describe the condition, but after splashing chilled water & bearing the sunlight on the face continuously it was darkened. This guess is after looking at the faces of others. Sun cream itself may have affected me immediately after putting it on my face. I used comb so many times. Due to rain and snow, some water droplets touched my hair when the cap or hat was removed. We cannot see organs of ourselves by looking inside otherwise I could describe it. The heart was working & I checked it at so many spots & events. Eyes were sleeping most happily. Goggle was sleeping covered with its small blanket in broken cover & therefore there was no load of goggle on the nose & ears. Mind tired. All became Mummy.

Don't even think that the body parts which are not described do not exist.

We awoke by a whistle. But we did not move. As usual, the dinner time was not our actual dinner time. It was time to finish the food. Some hours before after snacks, I was feeling too hungry again & it was the last food before dark. There was no option other than standing on a leg to move for dinner. It was a habit to share the plate but not the food item. After so many days I was eating Papad too with dal-rice. A person eating till last or holding the plate last had to wash the plate. The region covered with ice was near about 4-5 minutes. That chilled water of the same ice is still following us. As sunlight was brighter enough we unbundled clothes on the ground to dry.

As mud got dry there was a new design on a pant. I saved my expenses for new pants. In a very short time, all clothes were looking fresh. I sat on a green slope facing the sun. It was bright enough to close my eyes considerably. There was Greenery all around and a novelty in sceneries of cascades between beautiful mountains.

Amol was talking over a mobile. After his conversation, I made a call to mom. I cried while speaking with her at Nagaru & asked about dad & brother. This time mom gave the mobile to dad immediately. I had words only with mom after leaving home. Controlling my emotions I spoke with him & returned the mobile silently. Lying down in a tent I wanted to hear music. The body still needed rest but the mind was still wanted to dance. After so many days, I heard some music to refresh my ears.

We wanted to return now. In the beginning, we stayed for one extra day, which may affect the next plans. Most of the trekkers had booked their tickets for a return journey. Therefore group decided not to go to Bhandaktaj was one of the camps on the route map.

Group leader Kapil was asking two questions in each tent that anyone willing for Bhandataj & wants to have bournvita or not. We replied 'No' to both the questions together. To get one bournvita, one has to find a cup, then to walk for 20 -25 steps was a big effort that time. Without looking at each other everyone was speaking in a lying down position. Shreejith was satisfied that except for my camera nothing was lost till that time. We were waiting for dark. To complete the dream we have to see that dream first & for that, it was very important to sleep first.

Rest taken after a trek of 8-9 kilometers was making my mind ready for 100 km. We awaken on the next day when the sun was already moved far away for his journey.

Good Bye Dear All

After saying the very first "Good Bye" to the camp leader & Sherpas we started descending from Biskeri camp. We had to go down from 11000 feet to 7000 feet. But we did not remember how much km we had to walk. We already decided to avoid one camp surely & therefore everyone agreed to walk through another route than planned. Ways with turns and slopes covered with smelling mulch & greenery around remembering nature at Sahyadri Range of Mountains in Maharashtra. We said "Bye Bye" to the last snow when it appeared very small somewhere. When we were looking back we realized that we are descending a big height. So can we call ourselves Sherpa now? It will be better to be Sherpa in your own selected Field. No one realized the distance covered by him while chatting with friends. The very first person had to wait for the very last person to avoid someone gets lost though there was only a single way.

Slowly we got different reasons by everyone to reach to the home. Someone was eager to show all the photos. Someone was thinking about the next activity for his business. Some were planning for River Rafting. Some were wanted to pray at Manikaran after having a bath in hot water. We wanted to do everything. But any plan was dependent on trekkers lagging behind us. I could understand this because I was tenth from last this time. So people ahead were confused about their plans.

Till now, the first was known as First because he got publicity by all others. 'First' was just ahead of 'second' and so on. Hence, first should thank all others. Anyway someone was had to reach first. In trekking, there is no competition for walking. But everyone wanted to save time to avoid further problems in the next journey. Henceforth, we were going to deal with time, day, date, month, and year again & about to get involved in our world.

We were having ample time, but I was eager to have food made by mom. I was waiting to eat the fish & dishes made by mom. When we were at Grahan Village only, Khole Sir reminded me of one of the food items which my mom makes delicious. Since that moment I started remembering fishes we eat including pomfret, black pomfret, anchovy fish, wahoo, salmon, white fish, shark, seer fish, prawns, baby prawns, lobster, mackerel, Bombay duck & so many other 'friends'. Since we belong to Konkan, we have fish in our food frequently. Crabs must have set loose since I was away from home. Also, I had to return home because I have not eaten chicken and eggs and it has affected the 'Population of Eggs'. Actually, I was looking for a variety of delicious non-veg food.

I tried a variety of parathas after leaving home. It was the delicious food every time made with pure water, in fresh air & cooked by people with a great heart. Getting hungry after walking for 8-9 km there was no question about liking food. Our table manners were like a child who eats food moving everywhere. Sometimes we sat beside ewe or goats and sometimes with dog-crows. While eating with horses it was like a buffet. Every day, I was growing and it was my birthday. So that was a party every day. But still, I wanted to have lunch or dinner having seasoning, grated coconut, papad-pickle sitting on the floor with everyone chatting beside me. There was at least one item in a dish which was consisting of Potatoes to fulfill the need for carbohydrates for the body, but I didn't burp with satisfaction.

We had frequent halts after descending a lot. The group ahead was waiting for followers and moving further only after someone reaches them. The slope was so big that we could not turn our heads to the sides while walking. We could hear a sound by river & we thought we were closer to the village. We were saying goodbye to Cypress trees too while crossing the forest. The distance between two houses in the village was multiple to a distance between two trees in cities. Trees do not speak, but to protect the beauty of nature they might have fear about humans. Hence, trees were creating obstacles in our path. Many times people were changing their way when a tree with the diameter of the fallen trees was the same as their height. Leaves covered so many ways to make humans confuse so that they can't disturb biodiversity. Just due to the love with nature, trees here are providing a place to stay for so many rare birds.

Villagers were with us far ahead. A person walking ahead was an actual guide for everyone irrespective of distance. The color which I don't like, red, of the bag, was helpful to search the trekkers. We could hear a song of the river clearly but the village was far away yet. Legs were painting a lot. We needed slides like a day before which doesn't need energy at all. Most of the talkative trekkers were far ahead. So no one was with me who likes chatting. If found anybody, we could not speak with each other due to tiredness. After four-five hours walk, the sound of water from the river increased but I saw some plastic pipes also. I thought I have reached the village.

Increased Enthusiasm could not remain for a longer time. I could see 20 trekkers ahead carrying a similar bag. A bridge on the River was far away. That means distance till bridge, a distance on the bridge & again the distance from the bridge to the first person was to be recovered. In addition, the very first person was disappearing from the first turn. So I could not imagine a distance ahead.

Tough it was a plain way; I was not able to walk properly. Hard ways of cement started. It was obvious to complain about most of the things in our lifestyle. Life in the last days was so beautiful that we will be comparing our routine with those days in tents. If you get too many options then it becomes difficult to choose the best option. Instead of that by using fewer options life could be more beautiful. This was the learning from those villagers. Actually, Himalaya has given a lot & it was shameful that we could not give anything.

We saw some people & hear the sound of the engines. After so many days, I heard that sound & pleased my engineered brain. I was about to cross the bridge. That work was in progress. I was about to cross the bridge. As dust moved away a beautiful lady wearing a stylish dress and having long hair appeared walking on a bridge-like walking on-ramp. Traffic & heartbeat stopped. Instead of a signal system having red & green lights such a system can work more effectively. We were relaxed till she crosses a bridge. Tiredness went away & there was a little smile on my face. Dust increased gradually & no one was coming behind the dust. In a cold environment for 10 days, we did not even think about any disease but here I started sneezing continuously. I remembered my other deceases too. Neglecting all those was the best but temporary solution.

I came to the main road. I saw a hen, whose feathers were removed, whose smooth skin could be seen, walking ahead of me. Her walking style was similar to mine. I was confused about what to do? Shall I kill her and eat alive or cook later? Or shall I pursuit her to find a better hen or can I at least get an egg? I was looking at her hungrily. She realized a devil in me & ran away.

On the main road, I remembered that from here we had to go by vehicle then I will reach base camp.

We reached to Barsaini for Vehicle

Maybe everyone moved far away. I could see Kapil & advocate Patil only. As Kapil asked me I entered in a vehicle quickly. Dr. Vijay, Mr. Awasthi, Natu's uncle, Abhishek, Harini were in the same vehicle. All other went ahead for Manikaran. I had a guess. Vishal, Mukesh & Vinayak who did not come to a trance of Gandhiji will not go to Manikaran. I decided not to go to Manikaran to avoid delay only because of me.

The vehicle started in heavy rain. The road with potholes was having so many successive turns. Already body parts were loosened. That journey memorized me local transport in Mumbai. After descending for 6-7 hours, I was dreaming of good sleep in a vehicle, which remained as a dream only. 3-4 of us got down & said, "Goodbye" & we kept our bag on another seat & were relaxed. They didn't come to Base camp and left for another journey. I closed my eyes tightly & the vehicle stopped after some time near the steps at Base Camp. I was not having any amount. One of the friends gave money to the driver & extracted a promise for a beer from me. I agreed.

I was far ahead of my friends. I was not addicted to cigarettes & beer. I avoided drinks so my old friends were avoiding me. I remembered them accepting treats for new friends easily. Even I was also already thinking of celebration by the champagne bottle on the victory at surpass. I remember even Sachin Tendulkar also had champagne after winning the Cricket World Cup.

By keeping my feet on every step I stepped down to the ground. On the right side again there was the crowd for charging. All of them were looking like my juniors. Mithun Das in the reception tried to remember us & suddenly congratulated everyone. He took some photographs & we came to know that I was in the first group who came back to base camp. By coincidence, I was the first in any kind of sports.

I put the bag & shoes in tent number 16 besides the 15 where we were on the first day. We took our own bags from the storeroom by Mithun. The battery of the mobile was fully charged as it was not used & in a switch-off mode for the last 10 days. I called immediately to my mom & told her that all were safe in the whole journey & returned to the base camp. I had enough time to have a bath till all the trekkers return to the base camp.

Bearing the pain in both legs I reached from tent to bathroom. I was happy that today at least I will have a bath though it water will be chilled. I just splashed some water on ahead & tolerated it for seconds. As I poured it over my shoulder I started breathing fast. I waited for a minute. With an increasing amount on my chest & back, I started breathing very fast. It was courageous to have a bath. But still, I determined to bathe using soap. I could my skin and hairs only once though I wanted to clean at least twice.

All others reached to base camp. We got the signature on a movement card here, on which the signature of all previous camp leaders had signed. For all camps, Amol did this job for everyone, and only he was carrying everyone's card with him. We showed the movement card & took the official certificate from YHAI.

When I was returning my red bag, a new trekker on the ground congratulated us. They got motivated without any lecture. I tied up my own bag removing the snack brought from Mumbai. It recalled all the tastes which I was missing for the last few days. It finished quickly as everyone took it a handful. The weight of the bag was reduced by 250 Grams. I could guess my own weight was reduced by 3-4 kgs. We took leave from Suman, Abhiram & Vasant Rao in a big hurry. We did not stay at Base camp though we were allowed. We could get that official Certificate in hand from Field Director's hand in a campfire. But we had to leave the place. Going up to the steps again we came to the road. While returning from the Manikaran, Amol enquired about the bus & had immediately reserved seats for all.

11th May 2011, it was 6:30 pm. A bus by Punjab transport stopped near the camp of the Youth hostel. Two ladies asked "are you from Maharashtra?' I replied loudly & wished them for their trek. They were waving hands.

Our noise while entering a bus was ridiculous for regular passengers unaware of our victory. Singing loudly we started moving to seats at the back so that we can sleep there. So passengers started complaining to the conductor as we were not sitting on reserved seats, i.e. just on the back seat of the driver's. The bus started with successive turns only. First of all, I removed full pants & wore half pants on the bus. I left the seat for two persons from the left of the bus & shifted to a seat on the right side of the bus where three persons could seat. At some distance ahead we bought two big packets of wafers & cold drinks & celebrated like a party. I sent SMS to some of my close friends & relatives about the successful expedition of the Himalayas with YHAI.

'Youth Hostel Association of India'…I am so thankful to this organization. I have experienced very pleasant days in life. I felt so happy and proud sometimes when I born, when I joined the school, college while getting my first salary, many times. But it never happened that I am enjoying consecutive 10 days & credit of that goes to Youth Hostel. The whole team including workers, camp leaders, cooks, trainers, and management taught us lessons for discipline through their work and behavior. It's a challenge to create tasty food for everyone who reaches here from a different region of India. There was no shortage of food at any camp. Along with the tiffin we carried dry fruits, chocolates, toffies from every camp for having a taste on the tongue which was also keeping mouth wet. Everyone was so alert about the cleanliness. It was a little crazy for me for doing an arrangement of Electric bulbs for Campfire which shows their love for nature. They were so punctual about switching off the lights at 10:00 pm. & everyone will be on the ground at 6 a.m. It was actually boring for us to do any activity on time & systematically, as we were on privilege leave; but at the same time, we could realize its importance for any trek.

Their discipline about carrying the weight in a bag helped me a lot. Otherwise, it could be difficult for me to carry the extra weight of a sleeping bag from Ratapani to Nagaru. In the beginning, no one got injured while practicing rock climbing & Abseiling & till the end even after while climbing the ice wall. Medicine occupied space and given extra weight & wasted throughout the trek.

When we were walking on snow in a good atmosphere we realized that the sudden decision of descending from Ratapani was right considering the chances of bad weather. Reduced number of trekkers also helped in management looking at the number of tents ready at the Top. Those tents were built ready to face the storm for the next 30 days. People from different fields, behavior, classes were treated equally. Religion, language, caste were not considered at all.

It's a special feeling to have friends in the different corners of India. A narrow-minded approach enlarged like Himalaya. We were looking for higher dreams. We were thinking about the next plans & location to visit including Andaman & Nicobar Island, a desert or Rajasthan, North-East India, or island at Lakshadweep. Till now we were speaking names of the other countries & continents only for a business or honeymoon but we were easily speaking about Alps Mountain range, Forests in Africa & Antarctica continent.

Thinking about bigger plans practically money lowered its importance. We achieved enough confidence for the proper utilization of money. The most important thing lesson we got how to live life & actually how beautiful the current life is. It was the learning by looking at the lifestyle in the village.

It was 10:30 p.m. at night. We were too hungry. I could see that hen which came across but the bus stopped at a vegetarian restaurant. We asked the conductor about a no-veg restaurant. He said that will also be available here. Nair's uncle & his group who left the trek at Ratapani met us at this restaurant. We shared our beautiful experience with them & they were also happy after river rafting. While giving an order of non-veg dishes we were looking to the kitchen and food plates greedily. We returned one Mangala out of two after identifying it as fake. In a very short that one piece of chicken covered with spicy gravy got served in a dish, very next moment it touched my tongue, passed through the throat, and rested in a stomach. Every bite is pleasant and special when you get non-veg food in a veg restaurant. I break a so-called fast and after so many days I ate a lot & sang with a long burp.

Night of 24 Hours

After finishing all, we entered the bus quickly, which was too lazy for other passengers waiting inside only for us. Even we wanted to sleep without any disturbance. Mukesh asked for pain relief spray for his cramped leg. I remembered I asked him for sunscreen only once. He knew that I was also having another tube with me. But whenever anyone offers something to anyone Mukesh was deliberately requesting to give that same thing to me, especially sunscreen. This time it was my turn to tease him, but I could not find that spray. I started removing things in bags one by one.

And suddenly ….we heard a bang!!! The speed of the bus suddenly became zero for fraction of seconds & again it started moving without the engine's noise. But now it was going in the wrong direction. It was totally dark outside. The location was 14 km away from Sunder Nagar & heading towards Amritsar…at 11:30 p.m.

A small mountain on the left side & road was having turns. There was no slope on the right side but we guess that bus is going towards the valley.

Some mishap is going to happen….or happened already…..no…nothing will happen to me….nothing to anyone……Bus is going downwards?…..no driver is looking experienced…..he must be local…….nothing will happen……..but the bus will stop or not…..When diesel will finish it will definitely stop…no jokes please……….what will happen to my mom-dad-bro?…..what about dream home?……..possible without me ?……..or they will get cheated?……...please no negative thoughts ….. ….till now I have not done wrong to anyone……but I have hurt many times to so many….insulted many in front of many……..but I have done good work also…..was that not enough ?……….anyway……will see what happens……..5 to 10 seconds………ready to get injured anywhere………. Too many thoughts impacted at that same time?

Thoughts were jumbling in my mind & the bus stopped…

Alas! ……..it was an accident……bus stopped by stones placed at the edge of the road…..bulbs inside got switched off automatically……..all stepped down….objects in my bag fell outside on bus floor & some on the seat. I put few things in a bag as fast as I could. Bus-driver or an old age person sited behind Bus-driver was groaning "Waheguru, Waheguru". His pains can be felt & I still remember them while writing. One voice was matching to one from my group…….maybe Aswant? I decided not to go out without taking them out. While putting objects in a bag, tiny pieces of glass got collected along with those objects. Pieces of glasses were fallen up to the seat ahead of my seat which was first from the backdoor. Standing on my seat, I kept one leg on the next seat ahead. I could not see Aswant. He stepped down, I confirmed. I returned. I wore socks & shoes. Till that time a piece of glass got inserted into my leg. I knew that there was no single thing with me as first-aid. Came down to middle space & I dared to go ahead to see those two persons. But ahead, it was so difficult to balance on pieces of window glasses & it would be faster help from the front door.

Amol went to the bus cabin for switching off the Bus Ignition. Vinayak was confirming that all were got down or not. I shouted to him to find a torch. I picked the possible no of bags. It was a risk to keep these bags on the bus at that too on the deserted place. As per Amol's input, the Bus driver was seriously injured and had a big cut on his Cheek and some injuries to the eyes because of broken glass pieces. The bus driver was continuously touching his eyes with his hand. Amol and Vinayak ensure the driver that, you are safe and having some minor injury and averted further damage to his Eyes. Amol & Vinayak was not injured. Rakes informed me that all others have some injury. Rakes himself was safe. There was a small wound on the chin of Mukesh & on Vishal's head. Aswant was having a slightly bigger wound on a chin & it was bleeding from Shreejith's nose & lower lip. Alphin was keeping a handkerchief below his chin. Someone told part of his skin near the chin was swiveling. In the switch on the headlight of a bus, everyone sat in a queue on rocks quietly. All were mentally and physically hammered, for which there was no medicine at this moment.

From the front door, Amol & Vinayak were removing one passenger. I & one passenger helped them to lift. The driver was kept outside properly by someone already. The conductor was with big upset & was lost in his own thoughts. Passengers from other vehicles & the public were gathered around the bus. One shop owner came with Haldi Milk for the injured person. The car driver going beside in his car told to dial 104 for emergency help. Amol made a call and shared the exact details of Bus number and accident location. Without stopping near the bus none of the vehicles was moving away. We gave water to whoever asks. Someone offered us water too. I gave water to the badly hurt co-passenger & shown fake condolence. After doing some attempts also he was unable to move his right hand. Offered cotton to injured friends. I could not find spray for Mukesh at that time, but he found that in a bus & first it was used for me for my shoulder for a new injury. That was a bizarre coincidence, should not be experienced by anyone.

Slowly we came to know about the actual incident. As described by Amol, he was sitting near a window on Driver's side, after having dinner, Amol was seeing through the open window. Amol saw a big light source came exactly opposite to our bus and had a collision with our bus; Amol had witnessed the same through his own eyes. As per eyewitnesses, while overtaking one vehicle bus collides with the truck coming from the opposite direction at a normal speed. The bus driver could not be controlled his vehicle. The truck driver also attempted to avoid the accident....but he failed.... The mistake did by someone affect the truck driver's family.

As described by Vishal & others it was not only bleeding from the driver's body, but he was in a pool of blood. An ambulance arrived after 15-20 Minutes of Amol calls. Being severely injured Both the Drivers were given priority to get into an ambulance. When he was getting loaded in the ambulance blood was dripping from the cloth of the stretcher. He was counting his last minutes......second's maybe. Other injured persons who were behind bus driver and Alphin, Aswanth from our group; Amol & Vinayak went from the second ambulance. I, Mukesh & Rakes was taking care of all bags kept on the roads. While going to the hospital, Amol told that they had an encounter with a black cat that was lying on Road and their ambulance driver applied immediate brakes. Literally, one person came out of the ambulance to move the cat. Hospital is at Sunder Nagar means 14 km in the reversed direction from a current stop. We kept all the bags near the hotel. It was 12:30 a.m. at midnight.

We sited quietly on the steps of the hotel. I removed a piece of glass from my leg. Still, it was paining. I was doing frequent calls to Vishal, Vinayak & Amol. I was doing those calls to know their safety & they were calling us for the same reason. After some time, I started knowing pain in some more body parts. 2-3 Ambulance came again but we did not dare to go by a vehicle that moves at a higher speed than a bus. The cop came to the place of the accident.

At first, he had a post-mortem of nonliving elements, property. We requested a vehicle for taking us to the hospital. He ordered a cup of tea for us to the waiter in a hotel & told us to wait for his seniors. We were getting served for the first time in life from a government's account. He asked us the name, address. I got angry when he asked caste which is not at all relevant to the accident. I was listening to others & their caste very calmly. I was having doubt on a system in India, about treatment to the others as per their caste. I always criticize the system and I also feel a lack of knowledge about this subject of Caste. Why I was thinking about unwanted topics unnecessarily? It was a darker night for us.

Superior came & immediately he stopped a passenger

bus for us going back to Sundar Nagar. It was a courageous decision to go by bus then. There was no other option left. After keeping all the bags of 9 passengers we three & two co-passengers entered a bus.

This time, we were more alert than the driver of this bus. The driver was giving a lecture about how to avoid accidents, safety precautions, guidelines, general mistakes. The bus stopped in a few minutes. One more accident already happened. Victim & car driver were having a quarrel & fights too. I lifted my eyebrows and had knit to my brows. Bus-driver made a space between their vehicles & after some time it stopped again. That place was already seen where we had dinner a few hours before. Now it was the time of dinner for the passengers in this new bus. It could understand that for 1.5 hours there was no hotel after we had dinner at the hotel, yesterday in this hotel, but as this new bus reached here at 1 o'clock for a dinner that means in opposite direction there was no hotel at a distance of 3 hours? Why I was thinking about unwanted topics unnecessarily? I kept my eyes closed and started remembering the Himalayas before I will think more about the accident. But I could not remember it properly.

Mixed voice of driver & passenger, the touch of a piece of glass inserted in passenger's body felt while lifting him, his attempt to move hand faces of friends, the sound of Ambulance, lights of vehicles not allowing to remember any good thing. The bus stopped near a hospital. We thanked the driver & taken our luggage. Frustration could be experienced by anyone's voice.

Within this time, tickets for Amritsar to Delhi and the return journey were canceled. By Amol by sung Alphin mobile, this was supposed to for out of battery. Actually, we decide to go ahead by accepting the challenge given by the time. But Alphin got stitches to his chin and it closes our next plans. We missed a golden chance to visit Golden Temple at Amritsar, the program at Bagha border & Jaliyanwala Baag, which all are very close to our hearts.

As said by Shreejith we did not lose anything other than a camera but we lost enthusiasm, confidence & energy. Suddenly these were replaced by pain, laziness, and worry. We had to spend the whole night in the government hospital. A piece of glass inserted in a foot, made my one wish came true. I had two injections to my hip. I saw a bandage tied on the passengers' faces & remembered that his face when the big-sized glass was in his face near an eye. He did not sleep. The conductor was still in a big shock. The bus driver was not in that ward. As per Amol, the Truck Driver first has given Stitches in hospital, His left shoulder was totally dislocated and the bed in which he was kept is totally bloody and blood is continuously dripping from the bed. The doctor was stitching like he was sticking some Torn Cloths with needles. After giving First Aid, the truck driver was shifted to another Superior hospital. Last few days we were getting awaked at 4-4:40 a.m. & that day our sleeping time was 4:30 am. I closed my eyes. Anyway, with open eyes, we could see only darkness in hospital lights.

The next night, Pride by Painful muscles got hurt by accident a few hours before. Alphin, the most injured among us, was in a big sleep. Till yesterday we all were 'enjoying' river water to get fresh at that time. Today, we were using tap water one after one and splashing water over our face which could not make us fresh. We had to restart to enjoy from zero which was far away. I remember zero pillars at Nagpur.

When we were in our Sleep, Amol was awake, he had seen one more case of an accident in our absence at around 2:30 am in night, one couple came to the hospital, they were in the '50s Age group. They had met with an accident of won Car. The Husband was seriously injured; his white shirt totally became red because of heavy blood loss. Again the same doctor came for his rescue. Even after this condition, the person was able to walk on his own. Same time the officials of the Punjab Transport Team came to see the injured Bus Driver and enquired about our safety through Amol. They also confirmed that they will drop us wherever we want to travel till Delhi through their Bus with the Yesterday ticket.

Amol was ensuring that all were having sleep and he hardly able to take sleep for 30 -40 Minutes and that too at 5:30 am in the morning.

The next day in the morning, as Alphin & Ashwant were injured among us, they got admitted to Hospital yesterday. For Leaving for Delhi we need to take the discharge certificate from the hospital. For that, we have at least knocked 4-5 doors of that Hospital, which was totally new for us. From this place, Delhi was at about 10 to 11 hours. We were waiting for the bus since 8 o'clock, which was scheduled for 9 o'clock. Alphin got a green signal from the hospital & we came near a bus stop. We were sitting on a step at one shop in a queue. People were looking at us in such a manner that beggars came to travel or travelers became beggars. Sitting with tired posture & big bags, goggles, hats, shoes; had not a proper combination. We had a breakfast of 3-4 bananas from the shop sitting on those steps only. In addition to that, Amol has managed to arrange the Milk with Haldi for all of us.

Bus reached. Our journey started by showing the tickets for the previous journey. While entering that bus Alphin & Aswant declared their separate program. Their bags were with Amol who already entered a bus. I got angry with Alphin & Aswant when I came to know this after catching the bus. Leaving that topic, I was waiting for a proper seat. We had to stand for a longer time.

This time road was known but unwanted. All came near Window and positioned with a camera to take a snap of place of accident. Bus & truck were there only after their Clash. The truck driver passed away early in the morning & here truck was also upset. Our bus was quiet & placed her head on stone at the edge of the road. Pieces of glass were in the surroundings. After one more turn, we came to know the depth of the valley & how lucky we were at that time!

Death was so close. Death is unavoidable but the way of death should be an individual's choice is my thinking. If death is to be faced during a war or during asleep or while laughing, then I will welcome it. I chose the seat at the center of a bus and just decided on the safest seat. As we got saved in an accident we had sympathy for others. After a small request, we got a place to seat. Indians adjust easily in public transport. I remembered the crowd on a bus but when we were moving to Manali from Delhi and singing songs. While going towards Himalaya the music was so enjoyable, but now a person sited beside my seat was playing one song on a loudspeaker repeatedly. I could sing that song after some more repetitions. We ordered Aaloo Paratha (made by a potato) in which the potato was missing. We complained to the hotel manager, but it was too late. That day we had fewer 'carbohydrates'. I enquired with the conductor about how much distance we will have these big turns. He answered, "two hours". I was not afraid of turns. Accidents are common but having an idea before the journey makes your mind ready. Due to an accident yesterday, the trekkers who had victory became normal passengers in a very short time. The conductor was showing mercy as he was having little idea about us. Instead of going to Jalandhar, we got down to an unknown place from where we can go to Delhi on our own.

It was around 12:30 p.m. The temperature was around 35°C at Kirrtapur Sahib.

The day before yesterday we were experiencing a temperature of 4°C. Now, Sweat started running down from everywhere. Small trees had taken place in a shadow below big trees. We were in the city so we were not expecting tress on the highway. We were looking towards speedy buses on the highway and feeling the fear. However, we had to overcome that fear by sitting on a bus again.

Looking at too many vacant seats we were pleased as we could sleep by lying down on the back. The conductor was also in a great mood. We asked about the time for reaching Delhi. He replied, "Just keep watching wheel". We couldn't get it.

I kept a bag on a seat ahead. I could place my feet on the adjacent seat but I did not want any disturbance from other passengers entering later. So I kept my legs on a frame of a window. Hot air entering the window forced everyone to close the window despite the habit of being in the open atmosphere in the last few days. Alphin & Ashwant reached another bus met after one hour at the Chandigarh bus stand. Amol coordinated with them and had continuous calls with them and returned their bags. Shreejith also left our bus and joined them. We were only six & not injured much, moving towards Delhi.

The bus stopped near a garage. Though I was sweating I was in great sleep. For a longer time, the bus did not move. But I was satisfied that it was safe at least. All my friends got down off the bus. I was not worried as they get down without any noise. I could not see the driver and conductor in one glance. I thought they might have stopped for a break. Some passengers were inside. For a long time, no air came from a window. That means friends, passengers and bus were at the same place for nearly 2 hours. As told by the conductor earlier, I saw one of the wheels got punctured.

The bus started again on a too-long straight road. Since it was too late, the bus driver was also overtaking so many vehicles. Hot air entering in bus was irritating. The bus stopped near some local shops. The dish was so tasty that so many flies were having food on the same plate like we were having dinner at nights at various camps. One hand was used to hold the dish & one for waving to say goodbye to Flies who were not interested to leave their camp. Others having their one hand free ate more than me, I observed. A boring journey started again. Potholes, speed-breakers & brakes did not allow us for proper rest. We could rarely read the board on which distance till Delhi was mentioned. If we could read it then that distance was not motivating at all. Sunflower on the right side was looking at us with a smile & those on the left side were looking sad.

The speed of the bus lowered between 9 to 9:30 p.m. So many vehicles were stuck on a road. Though we were on a leave, the world was still busy in their routine work & some were returning to homes. The interval of movement by bus was less than the duration of being stable.

Amol told us to be prepared for getting down. We got ready and didn't get down. This happened at least 6 to 7 times. So, we thought he is still muttering during sleep. It was the time when we actually reached Delhi around 10:30 pm. By looking at our clothes & luggage Auto Rickshaw driver made a circle around us.

Dealing with Drivers in Delhi was the same as that in Mumbai. We had to go to the hostel of "Youth hostel Association of India" at Chanakyapuri. The actual location of Chanakyapuri was unknown to Chaanakyas of both sides. Rent of Rs.200/- was decided first. When we were reconfirming it, it was for one vehicle from our side & for a single person from the driver's side. Getting down from Auto we started walking. After walking for half an hour, we reached Station Kashmiri Gate for taking the Metro.

Thanks to the inventor of escalators. There was enough light with air-cooled & conditioned cars of Metro train. Proper arrangement of seats, enough space to stand & move good cleanliness, continuous importance & announcement in the clear sound system were the specialty. Journey in the metro was the motivation for the next days. A few days before, we were taking the support from anywhere to reach the higher elevation. We didn't stop permanently. When we were descending with huge upset, suddenly we were energized and reached the top. Keeping these things in mind we were waiting for the better tomorrow.

But before that, we were waiting for an auto-rickshaw from Racecourse to Nyaya Marg. We all six entered in a taxi & broke the rule. Thus, we became localities of Delhi, which was simple for us being localities from Mumbai. Both are Indians & are my brothers as per our pledge.

Taxi reached the Hostel. We reconfirmed the place before entering a building. We were happy with the affordable rates to stay. Avoiding lift due to its limit I chose stairs and putting a step one by one reached to the first floor. Beds were waiting for everyone. At 12 o'clock midnight I had a complete bath in my usual normal way by using water having a normal temperature. I wore clean clothes on my clean body & hugged to clean flat soft white bed. Each part of the body rested & finished a night of 24 hours.

Restart and Recall

13 May 2011. A new day in a new city for a new journey started to live a new life. Laundry boys knocked on a door and awaken us. The rate of laundry at Bhandup, Mumbai was Rs.3 /- which was Rs. 15/- at Delhi. We accepted as we only were aware of how dirty our clothes were. The laundry boy was should admit all our clothes in ICU. I was a little confused about how to inform about an accident at home. Before an accident, I already conveyed that we were going to Amritsar. Instead of putting the family under stress it was better not to inform them and let them remain happy & I will also live happily here without frequent phone calls, I decided.

Clock decided to have breakfast before 9:30 am. After so many days, we had breakfast with a discipline-keeping plate on a chair. We had bread & jam, juice, a good banana & tea. We had a complete breakfast pleasantly, of course, comparing with the only day before.

I took the newspaper. It was old, 2-3 days back. I started reading it considering it as today's newspaper only. In the last 15 days, we were feeling a change within us, but the world was the same. The biggest surprising old news for us was the Death of Osama Bin Laden. There was one news of corruption as usual & inquiry of old corruption was still continued. Murder, suicide, rape, kidnapping were the usual crimes but at different locations & by different names of victims. Instead of looking at social problems in-country, the focus was on the personal life of celebrities on the front page. Article & news, the tragedy of farmers, workers, and people affected by government projects, who did not get justice, yet, were in the middle pages & at a corner. The newspaper was looking like an advertisement paper since importance was given to the advertisement by more space, colorful pictures, and big alphabets. The future of billions of people was classified into only 12 groups under Horoscope. Is that mean only 12 types of incidents happen in the world? All are busy solving so many problems already however one more puzzle was given must be considering unemployment in the country. Others don't get time even for voting. A small cartoon was shown in a newspaper which generally makes you think than laugh. In short, the whole newspaper was a cartoon or joke or tragedy of the country.

We came out of the youth hostel. Traveling by vehicle was not our motto but we wanted to see Delhi in detail. We started walking on a side of the road though there was an empty corridor (this is the habit of the public in Mumbai). There was slight curiosity while walking in front of embassies of different countries, as I was totally unaware of those constructions. It was the first benefit of choosing to walk on roads. Out of many embassies, we all liked the exterior of the embassy of 'Bhutan'.

Both legs were having pain but we were praising ourselves for the kilometers we walked. Actually, I still had a doubt that one of the tiny pieces of glass was still in my foot. After the first impact only on a shoulder, there was a dark green mark. Without an exercise of shape at top of the shoulder was increased. Humidity at Delhi was forced to drink water frequently.

We reached to Railway Museum by walk. We rested for some time & observed that the toy train is taking a long time. In a very short time, it returned to its origin. We didn't want to stop so early. So we started walking again near to different railway engines.

The engine used to reach Matheran hill station, the Engine of the train in which SayajiRao Gaikwad traveled & some important railway engines were seen. The diameter of the wheel of one of the engines was nearly equal to my height. I was standing near a wheel and told someone to capture my photo so that I can tell this to others. I recalled one trunk of a tree which we crossed to move ahead. After a long break, we used a camera. We liked some engines & tried to handle some parts with care. Before going to one hall we read a rule not to stand in or beside a cabin of an engine, which was broken already by us. We were talking about one of the songs in the movie 'Fanaa' in which Aamir Khan motivates one of the Comedian Brijesh Hirji dancing on one of the engines imitating funnily Salman Khan. For that comedian stood over one of the engines.

Inside, there was a Sectional view of an engine showing the inner parts of an engine made us happy. Exact models of actual engines outside were just seen. Old tickets, old project, a technique of how the train changes the track, a letter because of which toilets are available in all train now, the contribution of the railway in independence, effective use by Mahatma Gandhi & photos of Railway Ministers till now, looking at all information we came out.

Pani-Puri seller Boy was waiting only for us. We 5, ordered 3 plates of Pani-Puri & like in Himalaya, around 3 plates we were 5, made a circle & started eating 'Chat' while chatting. We were not stopping to eat & he was not stopping to serve. It was difficult to trust with local people in Delhi as we experienced in small incidents. We asked him about the price. Though we ordered 3 plates and ate by 5, he calculated the amount for 5 persons, and asked for Rs. 75/-. That means the cost was Rs. 25/- per plate which for Rs. 10/- per plate at Mumbai. For a moment Mumbai is economically backward and we should also shift to Delhi for selling Panipuri. We gave him a lecture on honest behavior and suggestions to improve the quality of PaniPuri offering Rs.50/- & indirectly showed some anger.

Chandani Chauk, from here we were looking to different Delhi. Before that, there was vehicle rarely going with speed over Delhi roads but now all vehicles were moving with a speed of people walking beside. I could stretch my body while making space between people while making like in Mumbai in markets.

A picture is seen over one of the packets of Firecracker was in front of me. Tirangaa was waving on Red fort. I thanked every red brick from which the whole Red fort is built just to keep Tirangaa always on top & condolence to those who have given their red blood for the nation. Looking at the size of the fort from the front we needed to concern about hunger. We went to Macdonald's & had lunch. How they get the same taste for the same item at different locations? They might be getting fewer complaints because of its homogeneity in taste & look.

Before entering to front we bought a book giving information about the fort & Delhi where 'a door was giving security to the fort. There was no crowd at the ticket counter, but the ticket counter & the bathroom were painted in red color. King of that time must be having great foresight; that these Forts will become tourist place later rather than people will get inspired from History. It was the very first disappointing thing on the left side. Minabazaar got converted in the current local market which was expected to have an old look like before. I did not want to buy anything and motivate them indirectly. Most of the boards were in English that means we were not looking at any historic thing after purchasing tickets.

Museum of freedom fighters could replace our satisfaction after visiting Jalianwala Baag. A separate counter for that was far away that the museum could get close till we get tickets. One of the halls having old black-n-white photos of the red fort before repair and colorful photos after a repair was still open. On basis of those, we observed different parts of the fort standing in middle. There was nothing to see in Diwan-E-Aam and Diwan-E-Khas since Chhatrapati Shivaji Maharaj did not ascend the throne here. Since he did not sit there it was not even throne for me. We captured some photos since this fort also belongs to so many other Great Personalities. We felt it more like a palace instead of a Fort. Maybe we compared it to the Forts in Sahyadri Range at Maharashtra.

Looking at the temple appearing near it we moved towards Jumma Masjid. There was one alley, from where we entered to see Masjid. After walking 15-20 steps we were near a place where cleanliness, neatness was not known to anyone. A school in graham village was much better than this. We had to select the spot to place our foot to step up towards the masjid. Instead of blaming further in any holy place and making our mind negative, it was better to avoid entering the holy Masjid. We blamed people & hawkers around the masjid. We chose another way & moved to Metro Station named Chavadi Bazaar. At one turn Masjid was looking beautiful & clean. We prayed & went into one more alley.

This time I remembered allies in Mumbai & realized those are better than Delhi. Even I am also a king living in a palace. Because here row houses with two floors were so old & looking like not maintained at all. So many shops of used rusted spare parts of vehicles were on the ground floor. Electric wires appearing everywhere must be confusing the current from which wire it has to pass. It recalled our arrangement for charging batteries at basecamp. This is the only thing getting could remember and can be described. Nameplate, various boards, and banners had covered most of the vision. We stepped down for the underground Metro. Suddenly it was beautiful to keep your eyes open. It was so a pleasant journey from Chavadi Bazaar to Kutubminar. Instead of Delhi, we decided to visit selected Delhi.

As expected, Qutub Minar could be seen from a longer distance. As we were reaching closer we realized its height & hugeness. But the importance of Qutub Minar & Iron Pillar made by pure iron could not satisfy our curious minds. We did not praise that Minar. No one was allowed to roam in place around Minar in the evening. We could not get a reason behind this.

That day, maybe we were having negative thoughts. An accident & wasted day affected our approach & we praised those things too which were actually good, better, best. We had to spend some time in Delhi to get adjusted. Hot air all around for a whole day & buying a glass of cold water frequently from hawkers were the new things. Since drinking water was not anywhere there was a big business of selling cool water. There was no sign of change in this situation. As we were here for the first time, we did not bother about names with Old Delhi & New Delhi. For us both are new. Delhi which we saw including Chandani Chauk, Chavdi Bazaar, Historical Locations, Metro station & expected imagined Capital of India had differences. There were still more places to be visited yet.

We made a plan to visit Agra & Mathura for the next day & planned to see the rest of Delhi the day after tomorrow. We wanted to have dinner in Maharashtra but since we were too hungry we went to Gujrat Sadan where we reached first. We had Gujarati Thali. Stomach satisfied when mind & tongue remained still waiting for homemade food.

We decided to walk till we will get an auto-rickshaw but after walking for half an hour we entered in Youth hostel. I could not understand the reason behind painting my leg exactly. It was because a piece of glass was still inside or because of walking for 9-10 km today. I had two glasses of cold water from a cooler near room where I need not give money.

The day before, we slept in a bed without observing our room where 8 members of YHAI can stay. Rakes left us in the morning only. So there were three empty beds. Two new guys were in a room. One bed remained vacant. One guy was in a deep sleep. I was jealous of him & thinking to get an opportunity to sleep without getting disturbed in a dream at least But on the next day, Bus was about to arrive at 6:30a.m. So we needed to wake up at 5:50am. We were having 5 hours to sleep.

Another new person in a room was talking loudly on his cell phone. He was from states in South India & while telling his longer name it was ending with 'n' or 'm'. After telling his name he told his qualification also without asking, which was a long list. At YHAI, we were told not to tell & here designation. Because it differentiates everyone from each other and the person at higher post expects respect and the royal treatment of others. Some of the surnames are made on basis of profession. I remembered it and decided to follow the same rule when I will arrange the next treks at Maharashtra. Was that man looking for the same respect?

Anyway, while speaking on mobile he was frequently looking at my leg due to a change in my walking with a limp. I told him a short story about the trek & accident after he enquired. I put my mobile for charging & after returning from washroom I could not see my mobile at the same place. He kept my mobile below a pillow & was asking my friends if somebody has left a mobile deliberately. I asked for my mobile. So he started giving me a long lecture with loud. It was looking like he cares about my mobile more than me. Had I done anything wrong with him? I was unanswered.

I heard that he wanted to speak with Railway Minister. I could easily start my 'Word Express' but wanted to go to Car shed. Maybe his engine got cooled later.........maybe!

Waah Taj !!

Not because it was 5:30 a.m.; we awake to see the Taj Mahal which was seen earlier only on a box of tea powder, on firecrackers, in the book of history & in the movies.

Said Goodbye to 'ABCD', shouted me yesterday. I was happy that he was leaving the room and Delhi that day. We were waiting at the gate for the vehicle.

After meeting with friends at Chandigarh, Alphin & Aswant joined with us who were hurt physically only. Shreejith went to his workplace in Gujarat. We had not given advance to the travel agent. Bus, which was supposed to come at 'exact' 6:30 a.m. reached at 7:15 a.m. everyone in our group had a negative experience with travel agents in different regions in India. It was Rao Travels, started by South Indian for south Indian travelers as can be identified from their dresses & their language. Before entering in a bus he asked for Rs. 5,600 /-. He forced us to hurry in such a way that the delay was because of us. We were confused when he was not allowing entering without getting the complete amount. We collected money from different pockets & then entered in a bus. Vishal gave the final amount & we sat in the AC bus on the very last seats.

Journey started. The cleaner of the bus, 17-18 years old boy, was serving water bottles. Two bottles were less. We were waiting for water but as he neglected we blamed him as he purposely kept some bottles for himself. We accused him of corruption. He was not looking simple in nature but since we were seven he has to shut his mouth. The bus started running on Delhi roads. Due to wide roads, there was enough space for four sides of a bus which was very big for me as I had never seen such a picture in Mumbai. Because of the AC bus, Delhi was not hot today. We need to complete our quota of sleep. After two hours vehicle of Rao Travels stopped near a near south Indian hotel. We wanted to have local food and the cost of those items was such that even south Indian passengers also thought a lot before entering a hotel. They did not have any other options at that time at that place. We had one sandwich by one of the hawkers & one full glass of juice of Sugarcanes. Sunlight outside was too extreme to stand outside. So we returned to the bus & waited for others.

The bus started in speed. Kept my eyes were closed as there was nothing to see other than bright sunlight. One guide came to the front and announced that we are going to see 'Agra Fort' in few minutes. In our whole plan of the journey, this spot was not discussed. Now we wanted to see the place where King Shivaji was trapped & from where he escaped smartly challenging the security system by Aurangzeb. I was so eager and happy. The bus stopped & we came out of the bus; tears stand in my eyes as I saw a statue of my king riding on a horse and attacking the fort. Tears got mixed with sweat very fast as it was a sunny day.

The guide of Rao travels was waiting for all passengers after getting the entry passes. At the entrance, there was a 6.5 feet wall to both sides of a passage. Though there was no instruction to form a queue it was formed naturally since shadow by one wall in a passage was enough for a single queue. Rarely one could dare to walk outside the shadow. If someone found walking in Sunlight was having either very White or dark black skin.

Later we could see different structures in campus Fort. A palace with a green garden could be seen in one glance if we stand at a longer location from one corner. 'Do not touch flowers' was written on board, when there was no single flower at that time. We came to a palace with the guide. At a particular height, there was a seat for the king. I compared it with the TV serial made by art director Nitin Desai on Chhatrapati Shivaji and guessed the spot where he was said to stand. As I turned back a large view giving the same experience that I was actually in TV. I praised his work after recalling that episode.

South Indian passengers were confused and talking about the incident of Afzalkhaan which happened at Pratapgad fort which is at Maharashtra. Since tourists were speaking a lot, the guide was quiet. We asked him about the place where Chhatrapati Shivaji was placed under house arrest. He said the completed fort has occupied land with the shape of an alphabet of 'D'. A semicircular portion of 'D', which comes under the Defense area where that jail is. We got upset. We also did not show any respect to the throne of the king. Each wall, each pillar & precision in similarity maintained among them were so wonderful constructed by Nitin Desai of that time.

A golden dome on walls of white marble was looking so beautiful. People at that time must be avoiding leaving the fort because of the green garden & fountain. At that time Women were not allowed to go out. Hence 'Meenabazaar' was formed only for their shopping. We were looking to that Meena bazaar on the ground floor from the first floor & reached the beautiful jail where King Shahjahan was under house arrest by Aurangzeb. It was not allowed to go inside since chains were tied horizontally. So we were standing near the room. Sunlight was so bright and must be the same as that time; hence this jail was looking so beautiful. I had never heard about such beauty. If it would exist many politicians will demand such jail only if systems will be successful to prove them guilty. I wish I will be in such a jail from where I could see the forts of Chhatrapati Shivaji or the mountains of the Himalayas. Anyway, other than Tajmahal there was nothing to see.

We were standing beside another room from where also Tajmahal could be seen with Yamuna River taking a turn. We came out of the fort chatting with each other. While returning out on the road, the front view of Chhatrapati Shivaji's statue was looking in an attacking mood. If he will be in the same position continuously which mad enemy will dare to answer? I removed my hat & bowed towards him from bottom of my heart.

A journey by bus started. Sun was blazing down and can be experienced from the windows of the AC bus. To cover those windows with curtains cleaner boy came near our seat. We also covered those windows and teased him about those two water bottles. He was not having the answer. So we purposely opened those curtains again & started laughing.

We thought the bus started moving towards Tajmahal, but it stopped near a shop of beautiful handicrafts, as already declared by the guide. As we went inside there were so many things, utensils of marbles. It was actually a joke laughable when we see Tajmahal was used as Keychain and so many small models. Shajahan had cut worker's hands so that they cannot construct the same construction again. But Instead of cutting hands, the document about the construction Shahajahan could be kept confidential. (Perhaps this was also one of the reasons Aurangazeb put his father under arrest!)

Inside, they were selling and showing saris made at Agra itself. Being male having no girlfriend yet, Kela Silk, Badam Silk & so many types of Saris were for us. I ignored that hall & decided to come along with the person who wants those sari made in Agra. As I was about to come outside, I saw a Kutub Minar made of marble. It was so beautiful that one can say the worker has challenged two original things by the Art made by him.

After coming out of the shop, one poor uncle was selling toys. He was so old & looking very weak. That toy was made of Wires and it was hanging its shape after folding it differently. Alphin was also surprised & looked at me. I said, "It's really good, I liked it". He moved his head. Counting myself & children of relatives I bought four of them. Alphin & Aswant also bought the same & we got a discount.

As I feel I am out of the fund, went to ATM. Vishal & Vinayak saw the toy & came to the same uncle. This time there was one more, poor, younger person in a competition to sell the same toy with a reduced amount. Seller of toy taught us so many chapters of marketing.

Bus started. It was lunchtime. Again bus stopped at the costly three-star hotel. The specialty of this hotel was

South Indian Thali was available in Rs. 100/- only & condition to other dishes that those were having rates as per their Stars. Keeping the first specialty in mind & showing out attitude like condition over face we accepted greeting by the hotel manager & confirmed both specialties at the counter. Obviously Rice, Rasam was the main south Indian item in our dishes. Since we were having a habit we were putting hands in dishes of others too. We extracted each rupee out of Rs. 100/- very smartly while eating the food additionally we took saunf and lump sugar in good quantity.

The bus started again. He announced in a very short time, "Instead of Tajmahal we are going to shop where we can get the best sweet in Agra that is Petha". All other passengers opposed him till the time bus topped near the shop. We also get down and felt that travels had assumed higher expenses by all passengers and that's why he has stopped a vehicle to the small shop. On that afternoon time, no other shop was open. Travels, restaurant & shopkeepers were having very good harmony. Before buying the 5 boxes of sweets for Rs 600/- we tasted it & it was too sweet & the luscious.

Later, the bus was actually moving towards Tajmahal. An instruction was given to return before 5:30 pm at the Iron Gate made by Government. Mathura was yet to visit & yes, I forgot, we need to return to Delhi too.

There were so many 4-wheelers at the gate to drop tourists till the gate of Tajmahal in Rs. 10/-. All were struggling to catch the vehicle. Some were not moving at all. After some time, buses arranged by the government reached the gate which was taking Rs 5/- per person. Then the crowd started gathering to these government vans. Van was running full with the crowd. Including us, very few were left on road. We were six as Amol left us a day before at Red Fort to catch his train to celebrate his birthday with his family. 20 passengers could seat easily in a van. We saw a group of girls coming nearer to our van. Shahjahan inside us awaken & sited on a separate seat near window & was chuckling. Brother of Mumtajs, having a good physique, classified all Shahjahan on one side & Mumtaj on the other side of a van.

We forgot whatever happened with us since it was difficult to keep eyes towards anywhere other than Taj. Van was moving on a clean road bordered with green trees on both sides. The vehicle stopped & we reached the crowd at the original gate straight in front of the Taj. There were so many Shahjahan & living Mumtaj. Some were together & some were alone still in search of a partner. Observing the design on the gate we were moving with a crowd. Suddenly the crowd dispersed & after crossing the gate again there was a crowd; the reason was in front of eyes.

The Tajmahal. It makes you statue for some seconds when you look at first. Its size is such that it covers the entire space of your vision. So at the point immediately after the gate, there was a crowd. In the middle, the top of the Taj reflects in water in a rectangular tank beautifully. Trees on the sides of the tanks & grass on the ground enhance the beauty. That beauty pulls you more than pressure by the crowd behind you. You neglect whatever happens on both sides & anyway there is nothing to see on both sides. Instead of taking the photos from any side of the tank; I, Aswant & Alphin decided to step up on a floor to get the exact view which we have seen in different media. I was missing my camera a lot but my friends captured my pic.

Now it was time to go inside. It was a cool evening, the wind was pleasing. As we started moving ahead Taj was looking like a giant. Though there was an arrangement for keeping shoes aside, indiscipline Indians were keeping shoes near the corridor. A rain started. Will it be slippery walking over marble? Nothing happened. It was difficult to guess another end of the queue which was inside. Even we did not want to stand in a queue as we saw Vishal was very near to the entrance. We started chatting with him on any topic. He realized that we wanted to be in a queue. We were not stopping talk deliberately. Finally, succeed entering in a queue.

It was dark inside. Taking photos was strictly prohibited. A security guide alone could not stop everyone from taking the snap. Hustling in a crowd, I moved ahead to see what exactly people are looking for. There is a grave & it was decorated beautifully. As the whole Tajmahal was beautiful, this grave was also decorated beautifully. Someone especially a child may get lost here in the darkness. Later, we searched each other. We couldn't get why there was no arrangement for sufficient light considering children and elders. We came out of the back door. Yamuna River was flowing very calmly. While walking on slippery wet marbles I was thinking about some of the questions. For such a small grave why a huge palace is built? Why he had not given the gift when she was alive? Why did he use a large place, expenses, and a lot of time for one personal wish? If he was a king then after collecting tax he could do something for citizens. Luckily he had shown his love only for his wife. Otherwise, he could keep building big monuments with different stones & in next centuries ahead large space would get used only for tourism.

Rain stopped. Beauty in nature and weather created pleasant surroundings for couples. Suddenly, Mumtaj got hit by me. I turned around when her Shahjahan also turned & staring at me. I started walking like handicapped because already I was walking differently because of glass in afoot. That Shahjahan could remove the glass by removing my leg!

We had to reach near the bus at 5:30 p.m. We remembered this at 5:50 p.m. We started walking at a better speed. Looked back and saw Tajmahal again and said goodbye. We were waiting outside for vehicles which take fare of Rs 5 /-. There were Tongas too but I forced others to wait for the vehicle. I thought it was already late for Tonga to reach earlier than a van and giving Rs 20/- per person would be costlier for a very small distance. A horse could run well on the ground & a vehicle with an engine could run on a cement road. Sherpa could run well over a slope of ice for camera & I can catch the moving bus & train better than Sherpa.

Government bus reached to Bus of Rao Travels & we were the first who returned back. Now we were waiting for all others. There were one hawker selling handicrafts arranged systematically. He was shouting & calling to everyone going nearby him. His voice was cracking frequently maybe because of the profession. There are so many cracking voices near many historical places because of unemployment.

We waited for 45 minutes for the last person. Satisfactorily we stored so many images of the beautiful Taj. I remember all people, having a beautiful heart like Taj, & they are part of my life. With the same expectation ahead in life, we got mixed in the traffic of Agra. It was heavy traffic. There were so many people wearing dhoti-kurta, white mustache, eating a Paan & having little yellowish cloth around the neck. Suddenly I realized that I have entered one more state of India. So many people from this state have entered permanently in Maharashtra and in Railways. Most of the citizens are just getting advantage of the statement that anyone can stay anywhere in India.

It was just the beginning of the dark. Within 2 hours we were about to reach Mathura. I slept for two hours. As our bus was reaching closer, one more guide entered in a bus to show the temple & nearby places. He was so polite. His wordings were as sweet as butter. He alerted everyone not to carry a camera. He repeated this announcement about the camera so many times that I doubt he definitely knew that I have lost my camera. Getting down from the bus we started walking on the roads. On the right side, there was a big well having 20-25 steps to descend inside. The water inside was so dirty at nearer steps. Garbage was so old kept for so many ages. On the left side, there were so many photos of Lord Krishna in various postures imagined at his different age, shops of utensils, almost all kinds of utensils for worships & books. Butter in small earthen pots was looking sweet.

A guide stopped everyone along with him at one place & waited for everyone. Without asking he started explaining for a halt. Without going through the main road he took us from lanes. I remembered lanes in Bhandup at the time of the Ganesh Festival. In Bhandup also it is difficult to tell from where the queue will get formed, where you will see a statue of Ganesha & from where you will come out. At one entrance guards checked us for security. Only one person was going ahead out of two queues. After checking we all came together near a shoe-stand. We washed our legs at one tap one by one. As I washed my legs & turned back all were lost. Maybe I was lost......Yes; I was lost though there was no Cypress tree.

I stepped up in a temple. I didn't like the dark outside in alleys & bright lights in a temple. Were these lights were kept on purposely to show Lord Krishna that his attempt to enlighten human brains through Gita was unsuccessful? Everyone may be keeping his own battle of living a life aside while closing his palms in front of the statue of Krishna who played the biggest role in the battle of

Mahabharata. There were so many statues of so many other gods with their families. The Statue of Nine Avatar of Lord Vishnu was around the main statue. The main Statue of Krishna, Rukmini were so pleasant, alive & well decorated. As I had seen Tajmahal a few hours before a thought came to mind why Krishna did not build anything for his wife. At least he could write names of 16000 wives.

I was searching for others for some time, but it was difficult to identify anyone. I came near the shoe stand & confirmed that all are nearby only & seated calmly on the right side of the temple facing towards the shoe stand. I was continuously revolving my hat on my index finger like a Sudarshan Chakra. I was feeling that I am away from home for so many days. So many places were visited and so many are yet to visit. That leg was painting and it was difficult to know that is it due to a wound or due to continuous walking. I was pressing both the calves by own & saw all my friends coming near the shoe-stand. I did not have Curd in earthen pots since I was planning to celebrate the success by drinking Curd instead of beer. But they were praising it already. Putting shoes we came out. They did not like artificial jails made to indicate the location where Lord Krishna was born. When we came out but did not have any inspection.

All gathered in a bus and occupied their seat. A person speaking politely came inside & shouted "Kishan Bhagwaan Ki". All reacted, "Jay". He came near our seat & started asking for money for guiding us. I was lost in a temple so I denied it. He took money from others & before getting down he shouted the same. He joined our bus when all were unaware & later all came to know that extra money had to give him. So when he shouted again

"Kishan Bhagwaan he did not get a response.

This man had learned how to steal something from others. He could learn many other better & greater things. But he taught us a lesson on how to speak with people.

A return journey to Delhi started. After one & a half hours the bus stopped near a hotel. All of my friends were having a great sleep. When I asked for dinner, one voice was representative & declared that he was not feeling hungry. It was the actual time to have dinner after so many days. But there was no vacant seat & none of the items was likable for me. After a long time, I decided not to have dinner though I was hungry. I slept in my seat. At around 12:30 a.m. lights in a bus were switched on. We were near Delhi. Everyone was getting down at a stop where they willing to. We were not aware of the place. Driver stopped the bus at Nyaya Marg. We said goodbye to Bus & to Aswant-Alphin who were going to stay at a friend's home.

With heavy legs and counting each step, we entered in Youth Hostel. I was surprised watching ABCD in a room. After getting fresh I came into a room. Friends were still outside. Looking at me not walking properly, he shouted for not showing his leg to the doctor. He was irritating on a night at 1 o'clock. His mobile started ringing & he went outside.

That day one more elder person joined our room, age around 65 to 70. Nine years before he completed the SAR Pass trek. I told him proudly that I have done trekking in 25 forts in Maharashtra. He despised it. As I asked him what should be our next trek he said to stop trekking. He was listening to 'I am Barbie girl' on mobile in loudspeaker mode. ABCD told Vishal & Vinayak to take me to Doctor. We agreed with great speed.

It was a serious requirement to switch off the lights. Otherwise, these two old men would not sleep. I don't know when they slept as I was already in great sleep.

In search of God

Why a day raises every day? Last day of privilege leave. Have I taken longer leave? I am eager to reach home now. I have to wake up since Map in a book is still showing too many places to visit then we will depart happily for Mumbai. We got prepared before 9:30 am the next day. It's Sunday so more along with tourist local people will be also gathering at tourist place. We had a heavy breakfast.

We were looking at name boards of road. No one was walking on Nyay Marg, Neeti Marg, Panchsheel Marg, and Shanti Marg were shown in different directions. It is really difficult to follow Justice (Nyay), Ethics (Neeti), Panchsheel (Five morals), and Shanti (Peace). We reached near statue which we had seen at the backside of 50 Paisa Coin and to the backside of Rs.500 /- note. Followers of Mahatma Gandhi were walking behind him. I get someone's camera and told them to be in dramatic posture for a photo. But we couldn't get it either since this was also not possible for them who did not come near Mahatma's Tomb.

The parrot was laid down on the way. We 4 stared at him. He died already. At least we could keep his body aside; together we all bent in a waist to lift him without speaking to anyone. Vinayak lifted his hard body & kept it in a shadow below the bush. It's a small incident but according to my, it is an unexpected change in all. We felt he was one of the relatives of our friend who was singing happily for us in the forest in the Himalayas. He was a parrot who speaks well with others. If we saw a body of Crow we might not touch it all. You should be nice and sweet while speaking with others, I need to introspect myself.

While walking we were recalling each other to see parliament. But we missed that road by mistake. So it appeared little when we turned back.

We decided to go to Birla Temple nearer. Temple was not that much near for painful & tired legs. I was going very slowly. There was some discount on sunlight at Shadow. Ganesh Temple, Hanuman Temple, Shiva Temple is known, but why it is known as Birla temple?

That means will we see Mahindra Temple, Tata Temple, Ambani Temple, Godrej Temple very soon?

Running away from burning marbles I reached near tap. I washed my legs not because I was entering the temple but mud in the Himalayas was still in the cracks of my feet. I could realize 'Investment' while stepping up.

A religious construction is the only pleasant place where all the required facilities with the best cleanness, peace all exist together could be found together. A very poor person all donates Rs. 1 coin as belief or maybe superstitions or because of psychological pressure without asking for a receipt. Looking at the other side, it also provides an opportunity to earn something for artists and labor. A question comes to mind how we can create a whole world with an atmosphere like religious structures.

Joined my hands in front of Ganesha, Rama & Family, Shiva & Family; but I could not see god since my mother, father was at home & Chhatrapati Shivaji is in the heart.

I could get Coconut water before entering the temple. Others were already in a rickshaw for Lotus temple when I came out. We used a map & changed a line in Rajiv Chauk and got down at Nehru Palace.

There was one family preparing and selling 'Lassi', a milk product. We were also thirsty & hungry a little bit. The stomach needed something cool inside. We were expecting something homemade & ordered four glasses. They already identified that we would be ordering 'Lassi'. Each of the three was giving suggestions to everyone to make it better. Everyone churned it with churning staff one after one. They put malai & red cream over it. It tasted sour but we hid our expression not to make them upset & praise them. We had tea with the same love at one of the homes in Grahan Village.

Without asking the driver he was waiting for us to finish the lassi. We entered inside telling him to go towards 'Lotus Temple'. But he started to drive exactly in the opposite direction. We asked him for doing this so. He gave a general common reason for the longer route. He was actually lying he wanted to show Delhi Haut in the same fare.

At the entrance only a very big Tambora and so many rare articles with a little artistic touch for sale. My favorite Gramophone was available in a big size. It's a very good evolution from Gramophone to earphones till now. In the future TV may get replaced by goggles which will show the movies, I imagined (at the year 2011). There were so many tourists, foreigners.

The price of the same sari was Rs. 100 /- more than which was bought by Vinayak at Agra for his mother, So Mukesh canceled to buy a sari for his mother at this shop. As we go to a higher altitude amount of importance of Oxygen increase and the cost of Maggie was also increased to Rs. 60/-.

A chessboard having cost Rs 25000/- & was a special attraction. Each coin, a soldier was such big that players may feel that they are actually killing their enemy. It was a table of near 2 Feet in diameter. The height of the king was 3-4 inches. Most of the things were not affordable for us & some could not be inserted in a bag, so we didn't purchase anything. Rickshaw drivers were waiting outside.

Then rickshaw started moving towards the temple. Big Lotus in white color was looking beautiful from a far distance. There was not so much rush because of so bright afternoon. The skin was suffering a burn. Everyone was bending down completely just to keep sandals in a room. Such arrangement must have done to hide this arrangement which could disturb the view while looking towards the temple from any direction.

Vinayak & Mukesh were looking so bored of sunlight & sat in a shadow. With a paining leg, I kept walking with Vishal. People were coming out of the temple, but no one was allowed to enter. Two or three queues became longer & longer. Scout outside started informing us about Bahai, which was new religion for both of us. We were not listening to him as it was like a lecture in a school or college which we didn't want. Already we are having so many religions in India, so we were not interested to know about one more religion, which is the same as others, gives the known message to everyone and not followed by anyone that all are same. After few minutes all entered a hall. Everyone started discussing as those who came late were going with those who stood in a queue for a long time.

Everyone had seat inside quietly. For that benches were already arranged properly. We were in the temple expecting some statues but there was no such thing where we can face towards it and pray. A staff member told us a concept and to recall whomever as a god, till the possible time & then come out of temple peacefully. We kept silent for a Truck driver who lost his life in the accident. The only temple was watchable. The concept of god was presented in a different way & there were so many questions on many faces and some were muttering. There were rectangular tanks outside having a fountain which could be started in the evening. We could imagine our own view in the evening & night with fountain and lights as we could imagine a picture of God based on our thoughts and experience.

I took back my shoes from another side of the shoe stand. A man was appointed specially to remove the crowd from this side where everyone was wearing shoes. He was shouting at people. But a lady shouted at him so effectively that everyone wore shoes near the shoe stand till the lady was there. We came to the main gate & told Vinayak & Mukesh that they have not done missed anything special.

I think we can get peace anywhere and we cannot find it in a closed room too. It is dependent on the individual's mind. In a journey when there is a crowd singing a group song, you can see people reading a pray or students are studying with concentration. When children play in a park making noise when there is heavy rain on farms, inflowing rivers, waves of the sea, peace can be seen very easily.

Peace after Bhajan of God in a temple & peace before winning a heart-taking game, both make you stay focused. Not only that, we loved peace when we were getting tired while climbing on Himalaya & when we reached the top we shouted loudly & must be liked by peace. But we never want peace faced in an accident. But nobody wants Peace for a moment after the bomb blast & peace in some minds for a lifetime at many homes.

We got corrected while reaching Kalkaji Mandir station, which is nearer to Lotus temple than Nehru Palace. We reached our next destination i.e. Akshardham Temple station. It was written somewhere at a station that entry was allowed till 5:30 pm so we were moving fast suddenly. We called one of the rickshaw drivers. This was not an Auto Rickshaw. This rickshaw needs to move with peddles that could be easily found in Delhi but not in Mumbai.

Two sat behind rickshaw driver & two by touching back to their back. The rickshaw driver was so lucky. We reached her after reducing weight by a minimum of 3 Kg. per person after our trek. We had not a proper lunch yet in Delhi. Our entire luggage was kept at the hostel. Otherwise, we could easily show the meaning of weight. Even that road was flat. However, we still praise those who are driving this vehicle without covering a body in very bright sunlight in a hot environment.

The parking area was just like an exhibition of different cars. There were too many vehicles on one ground. It may be possible that the owner may exchange their vehicle without realizing it. But by looking at the luggage you can confirm your car, right? But why look inside as you can see a number outside on the number plate? We came to the ground with some illogical jokes.

Here there were so many queues. At one place there were four queues to keep mobiles, camera & bags. We observed it was taking a lot of time to move ahead, so myself & Vishal were in a queue at the canteen whereas Vinayak & Mukesh lined in a queue for keeping luggage. After half an hour we came together. Two samosas were on each plate & we were eating it like these were the last samosa in the world. We had only one bottle of water with us. Instead of standing in a queue, we shared a bottle with great understanding.

Then, we were in the main queue. It was a group of queues or queues of groups. There were separate groups for gents & ladies. As we were moving ahead people around everyone was changing every time. This is only because of the location of fans. All were trying to stop near a fan not for air but to hear the sound of blades since those were not working well. Everyone was running for fans as people run in a queue to see a statue of a god. There was a continuous announcement not to smoke & it may provoke smokers to smoke. That sound from the speaker was so continuous & irritating. That amplifier must be getting bored.

A group moved ahead & turned into a queue. The security person was doing their job by inserting a hand in everyone's pocket. A wallet was opened & shown to the guard. Everyone removed the belt. Wallet, belt, watch, and coins whatever in pockets was kept in a tray. For a long time, we were assuming that these trays are given for flowers, coconut. The collar of the T-shirt & folds of sleeves were checked. All were passed with zero marks. This was the biggest checking done anywhere throughout my life.

It was such a bad feeling that all are facing doubt in

their own country because of some of the devils having a human body. After crossing the gate we were not feeling secure as there was no door to the sky. Security was for the temple not for human beings, for devotees, and for tourists. But is it possible to provide such security?

If it will get provided then on what topic will be left for politics? Who will sacrifice his life for the country and who will create riots? Who will care with fear? Who will run with fear? Who will only speak about the security of citizens while seating at home or in rallies for election? Who will do corruption? How many terrorists we will keep alive? How many terrorists we will leave for passengers in airplanes? How many crores from pockets of crores will be spent for the security of selected citizens instead of all? How much we will be investing in defense sectors? Who will neglect this subject? For how many times we will face attacks? Who will forget this? Who will laugh? Or should not we laugh?

Akshardham Temple is beautiful from a far distance & as you go closer you can see details that are even more beautiful. No place was left without design. This temple challenged all the palaces, caves, statues, design & lights which I have seen ever at various places. Wherever you see, you will observe engraved designs with high accuracy. The statue inside was golden & beautiful because of the gold. That God was new for us. It was eye-pleasing lighting inside. After praising the temple a lot we were looking at playing sparrows in a temple. We mean me & Vishal.

Vinayak & Vishal were not bored of traveling but were avoiding crowds. We needed a rest a lot but at our own home. We all were aware of this. A way for going from temple to canteen was also made creatively. Outside &

inside there was a huge crowd. Our friends were seated somewhere away from the crowd. The bathroom was at the corner & drinking water was beside that. Water in a cooler has to have a normal temperature & did not have a good taste. It forced us to buy a water bottle. We already expected the high cost of food items. If an economically poor person will come to see the temple he will face a problem with food & water. That changes our mood and decided not to get into the trap.

My three friends were eating Chana-Masala & I stopped my movement immediately. It was an evening till we left a temple. Temple started brightening with lamps and started showing surrounding darkness. It was looking like a campfire at base camp of YHAI. We spent some time in a book shop and museum. We came out of the whole campus of the temple on the straight road which was beside a gate from where we entered. One of the gentlemen was arguing with the security officers about leaving him at the earliest in a temple. He was telling them that he has relations with many VIPs in the country. People passing near him were stopping with curiosity, so two extra officers were there to handle the rush. Though it was a small incident with respect to us we noted some more extra soldiers were looking at remaining others than a gentleman with very sharp eyes. Someone could get an advantage if security is focusing on a single citizen.

Can we save millions of money, a large area of land, huge electricity & priceless soldiers? Any project serving people could be implemented easily.

We reached the railway station of Akshardham Temple. All three started walking on the stairs. I considered them fool & stood on an elevator. I reached a platform where a train was going in a different direction than we wanted to go. As the train landed on the platform I realized my mistake. Before my friend could see me I stepped down & mixed with them showing innocence on my face. They were laughing already but luckily on a different topic.

Now we wanted to rest very badly. Legs were painting & were a looking part of daily life here. It was the last night in Delhi. When we reached India Gate on the very first day I wanted to seat in a beautiful garden in front of the President's house. Vinayak & Mukesh decided to return to the hostel. The remaining, both of us, we're still ready to bear the pain. We got down on a station of the Central Secretariat.

Two days before, we had journeyed in the metro by giving Rs. 100/- per person, to travel from any station to any station for the number of times. To gain a profit from this scheme it was needed to travel in such a way that total expenses in Metro should cross the amount of Rs. 100/-. For that, we went to the platform of the last station of Metro that was Huda City Centre without need. Today we were using a scheme in which we could get the remaining amount out of Rs. 100/-. We used both the schemes very effectively & very cleverly. While getting money back we awaken one of the officers in great sleep. Of course, he did a mistake while calculating the amount but twice.

We were in the middle of India Gate & President's House. The lighting around India Gate was so beautiful. We sat on the ground having green grass and could stretch our legs. After 2-3 minutes Vishal sat & stand immediately after bites by ants. I was seated very close to him & looking in surprise towards a person doing an exercise (rope jump) at night. Children were playing & 4 persons were gambling with playing cards below government lamp & looking so happy. After some time we changed our place. We were not much interested in the walk so we avoided looping one ground and jumped so many times and reached one of the vehicles. We were remembering our trek while doing so many small-small acts.

Nothing special had happened that day. But still, only one news reporter was giving a live telecast for his news channel. It's just like a security system; wherever you need it; it will not be available. Sometimes it is too boring to bear them continuously when they keep on running same the old videos or every small incident or sentence of leader as Breaking News. One vehicle with a red lamp on top came at a speed. The reporter ran towards the vehicle for news. The vehicle increased its speed after looking at the reporter.

As we sat there for a longer time. One soldier enquired about us. We answered that we were here to travel from Mumbai. His tone of speaking got changed and also showed a willingness to spend some time of life in Mumbai. He shared that people at Delhi enjoy from 7 pm on Sunday till 4 o'clock on the next day morning. People coming into a garden may not know him, but he could easily remember everyone & guess perfectly sitting place of everyone. For the demo, he showed the seating place of two boys who came in a red car before they leave their car. He proved his experience & found intelligence. We said goodbye to him & informed him that the next day we would be going to Mumbai.

We thanked Delhi Metro at race court. Delhi showed us Metro & Metro showed Delhi. Vishal wanted to walk again from race court to Youth Hostel so he removed a map from a small bag & started walking in the exact opposite direction. As an auto-rickshaw reached us we entered. Was it was my mistake that ABCD I was in front of him again.

I told him first and immediately that we had confirmed with the doctor that there is no piece of glass in the foot. By great coincidence friends also informed the same report. Today, I was a little upset to leave Delhi & the last day of Privilege leaves. I was happy too as I was going home.

Today ABCD was looking in a great mood due to the arrangement of his train tickets. As we informed him that we were leaving the next day morning he seated to chat with me. Did he start telling his daily program which started with his lunchtime? His mobile rang when he was telling his activity at 5:30 pm. My friends were laughing at me. Actually, they were also wanted to sleep.

We wanted to pack our bags at that time. Three pairs of socks used in 15 days without washing thrown away in a box. The weight of the bag got reduced. Snacks& pickle was eaten already. It was a challenge to insert boxes of sweets (Petha) bought at Agra. But some Pethas in one box bought by Vinayak was eaten, and then I decided to have fun with ABCD.

I remembered that he was telling his program at 4 o'clock that he takes a tea without sugar as he was diabetic. I purposely offered Petha in a box first to an old uncle who came the day before. I offered the same later to ABCD too. As he was talking on the phone he signaled with his hand to wait. I sat on my seat & had HiFi with friends. All we're waiting for the next fun. I was confident that he must come to tell his daily program from 5:50 a.m.

And the same has happened. While he was telling the program I offered a box of Pethas again to that diabetic patient. Surprisingly he took sweet of four different colors. I looked at him & blamed myself for buying Petha in 5 different colors. Purposely I showed him the color which remained to choose. He took the fifth one also.

And he started telling a program after 5:30 pm. As it was the luscious sweet I kept that box away from him on Vinayak's bed. He also changed his place & seated beside Vinayak. Vinayak was busy with his mobile & sending messages. ABCD was trying to see his mobile. After eating 5 sweets he inserted his hand in a box. His program was still continued & no one was listening. I was caring for sweets only. After eating 8 pieces he said again that he was diabetic & he finished his day & went out. By telling that incident repeatedly I packed my bag. I used Vinayak's box by mistake so I had to return him my unopened box.

We said goodbye to Delhi Night. Experience in Delhi was the same as in Mumbai. The public in Delhi faces the same problem as faced by people in Mumbai & the solution is the same, just wait & watch. Here too, an area where government offices exist, is clean, having wide roads same as at South Mumbai and at BKC. An area in Chandani Chauk & Chavdi Bazaar is like the Central region of Mumbai & the area till Noida, where construction work was going on, is like Navi Mumbai.

People here are having fun, busy & professionals, but while enjoying, the environment supports Mumbai. This was the small observation of Delhi in two days only. Of course, this city must be more wide, tall & deep than observed. We were waiting for the next day.

After leaving home we traveled by bus, Auto rickshaw, local train in Mumbai, express, all types of buses in Delhi, taxi, Metro. The next day I would be going on Airplane first time in my life.

The journey started in an imaginary plane without carrying a ticket & bag. The biggest question from childhood is how big an airplane actually & how it looks from the inside. The answer will be available the next day. There was no one other than me in an imagined plane. I found out a way in between clouds without a pilot and flew at a higher height in a dark. The body was on bed only.

First Flight Fun

As a new day dawned, it was time for a new journey. Today, after so many days I was going to meet my parents and my hometown. I wanted to tell Sahyadri that I had met Himalaya. I wanted to tell King Shivaji that I had escaped from Agra and won Delhi too. But I had not conveyed yet that I had faced an accident.

While traveling through Delhi, I was in a negative frame of mind. Though we reveled in the beauty of major historical places, the observation done was very less due to time constraints, in the Peak hot environment with painful wounds. I felt sorry for expressing negative comments for the Capital of India.

Our taxi had already been booked. The taxi driver had to search for 'Nyaya Marg'. Nyaya means Justice which is difficult to find in India. The driver found it difficult to find this road though he had been in Delhi for so many years. But we guided him on his mobile phone towards the Youth Hostel without referring to Delhi maps. He arrived after a while.

As the taxi hit wider roads, the driver hit top speeds, as it was early in the morning and there was hardly any traffic. But it was still not fast enough for us, whose minds had already reached home far ahead of us. The taxi finally stopped and we realized that we had reached the airport. I put my bag on a trolley. My walking style changed suddenly, as I did not want anyone to identify me as a first-time "Air Traveler". I walked with cultivated ease and confidence, despite observing everything curiously like a child.

Why were some people wearing a suit in such a hot environment too? Is it not boring to wake up early frequently for business? Which queue was for what purpose? Above all, where were my aircraft, and on which 'platform'? Hundreds of questions flown in my mind.

I had heard often that all things in the luggage were required to be shown during security checks, so it was boring to imagine unpacking and re-packing the whole bag again. But the bag was given to the security officer, kept on the conveyer belt behind him after checking the weight, and then the bag started its journey. I was worried. While traveling from Delhi to Manali I had put it on top of a bus on my own. What would happen in the case of planes?

We had breakfast in the airport though it was expensive. It was good because of the higher cost. In fact, it was really good. All of us had breakfast and lined up in a queue. I wanted to observe the expressions of my friends, but I was far ahead of them already. I was laughing when the security boy was checking me.
I had no sharp weapons with me other than words, and my mind. In Himalaya my mind was like a feather of a peacock, in an accident it was worn out, in Delhi it was kept aside and in Tajmahal, it was like a rose. Now it was going to fly like a kite, a thread of which was in hands of mother.

Listening to the announcement all of us moved towards gate number 19. We sat on empty chairs nearby, to practice sitting for a longer time! There were long queues besides chairs. We were not giving any attention nor neglecting them completely, because we knew the technique of catching running buses and trains but not a plane.

Passengers to Mumbai were requested to form a queue in front of door 19. We realized that a queue which we had been looking at for a long time was actually for our flight. I started moving step by step in a queue. Looking around me, I reached a glass door. Those who were ahead of me went away in a packed bus. As the bus moved away I saw 4 to 5 slightly bigger white sparrows in the airport. Binoculars were not needed to see them. They were white birds with a blue stripe on their side and their tail was also of the same color. One sparrow flew away and another was ready to move. Suddenly a bus disturbed my vigil of the sparrows and I went near a door on another side to take photos of the sparrows. A strip of blue color on the bus bore the word 'INDIGO'.

The bus stopped. I found myself walking on a flat surface in a helical path. As I was smiling continuously somebody smiled beautifully standing at the door of the aircraft. I was so shy that I almost died. Now I was hoping that the elder person behind her would welcome me considering myself as his expected son-in-law. But there were so many sons-in-law behind me. Mukesh, behind me and, we're looking for our seat. At the same time, I heard a pleasant voice say, "May I help you?" and music began playing in my mind. In a low voice, I said seat no. 23. Mukesh was seated near a window, I was beside him. Vishal was in front of Mukesh.

People were keeping their bags on the overhead luggage racks. They were applying unnecessary force on the door to lock it, while those beautiful ladies who were so clever and dedicated to work used their brains. The doors were closing on their own; blushing when the ladies lifted the heavyweights placed them in the racks with their beautiful hands.

Everyone was finally seated in his seat. There was enough light and air conditioning through blowers to adjust the flow of air. Everything was neat, clean, and systematic. As we looked outside, we found that our seat was right beside the aircraft's wing.

More than a hundred years ago, the Wright brothers had developed a successful working aircraft. So many scientists had earlier attempted to do the same. Saint Tukaram traveled by Pushpak Airplane to Heaven as heard in mythology. Ravana kidnapped Sita and took her to Lanka by aircraft. This meant it had been invented so many years ago, centuries before the Wright Brothers did.

Vishal finally found the knob to push the seat backward. He made a mistake by informing us of his discovery. Without demoralizing him, we congratulated him in the same serious mood. From that moment on, we had to endure his jokes for the next two hours as there was no other option because the door was closed.

The aircraft began moving and aligning itself with the runway for take-off. The pilot was announcing something over the PA system, but we neglected him as our sights were elsewhere. Suddenly we heard a pleasant voice. Now we were concentrating on every word being said. Another beauty started giving instructions with postures and gestures. Language without words was the best, I realized, as it was understood by everyone. She cared so much for everyone like an actress in a lead role in any TV serial, informing us about the seatbelt, oxygen mask, emergency exits, and life jackets. There was nothing else more watchable in the aircraft.

The aircraft was on the runway, calm, stable, and ready to fly. Suddenly we heard the musical drone of an engine. It began moving slowly and suddenly accelerated to a dizzying speed, as objects outside the plane began racing backward with the same speed, as if out of fear. The aircraft was cutting through the air, leaving the runway behind, as the ground became inclined and bent. It said goodbye to the earth. The aircraft climbed steadily at the same angle, and slowly it leveled out. After 10-15 minutes, we were allowed to detach our seat belts by the same sweet voice. Now I began moving around to see outside the window. As I was in the middle seat, this movement could be seen from anywhere. Each tree was looking like a leaf, bungalows like toys, flowing water like a piece of plastic.

Before I could identify any object, it was already gone way back, behind us.

Other passengers too, started moving around. Some were asleep, some were going to the bathroom, and some were talking to others. Many of them might have been also first-time fliers like me. A young boy was watching a movie on his laptop. He did not know how to enjoy a flight journey. Ashwant, flying for the first time, was also sleeping.

The scene outside was similar to the scene 3-4 days ago. It was white ice everywhere, the only difference being that we were in an aircraft. A crowd of clouds was with us for a long time. In a short while, two air hostesses were walking in the passage with trolleys carrying water and cold drinks. We had not celebrated our victory over the Himalayas yet. This moment and place were perfect for a celebration. Alphin and Vinayak were seated at different unknown seats alone but were in the same class. We asked for water first and 3 different cold drinks, one for each, with love. They gave us the same with love, of course. At this height, the beverages were not as cold as expected. I had heard the general method of selecting a girl for marriage earlier. It was similar to this. At the same time, the bright lady told us the cost of the cold drinks. She was good at business and polite too. Another lady was similar in qualities. Clinking our cans together, we shared our joy.

We were still having fun, passing jokes. Was the speed of the aircraft lowered? Over which city were we flying? Could we see the sands of Rajasthan? Where were the birds? How higher were we in comparison with the birds? Our questions were flying continuously. The Air hostess went to the front of the cabin. They were closing the curtains before having any communication within themselves. Maybe they were hiding their expressions. A puzzle was not solved yet. (Do they having the same feelings?)

Now there was a shortage of jokes. For the past 16 days, as we were continuously on the move, we could feel the journey. But now, we wondered if we were moving at all or not. We were quiet for 5-10 minutes and so close to Mumbai as we were instructed to wear seatbelts. Deliberately I decided not to wear it.

Looking through the window, a ship sailing in the sea looked like a picture on a tiny matchbox. Searching for Mumbai was a difficult task; I could understand the pilot's confusion. The aircraft's nose dipped. Though I had not tied the seatbelt, I was holding it in my hand for any emergency. As we flew closer to Mumbai, the Pagoda at Madh Island was seen.

While leaving Delhi, the earth was touching the feet of the sky and while landing, the sky was blessing her.

The speed of the plane seemed like zero, but suddenly it appeared to be extremely fast as the aircraft approached the runway. The seatbelt held loosely so far was now held tightly as I was bent forward at a sharper angle than the others. As I looked outside, the aircraft was parallel to the ground and the entire surroundings were speeding past us. Even before I could write 'speed', the aircraft would have covered a great distance.

Finally, the giant eagle touched the feet of my home state. Just a moment ago, I had worn my seat belt, and the very next instant; there was a jerk as the landing gear hit the runway. It was difficult to imagine to what extent it was experienced by passengers. After a while, the aircraft came to a halt.

The pilot informed us that the temperature in Mumbai was 30°C. After experiencing 0°C in the Himalayas and 40°C immediately in Delhi, 30°C sounded pleasant. I had to praise the pilot for landing the aircraft on the right runway in the right city, flying over the earth which was rotating and revolving around two different axes.

Everybody was in a hurry to disembark. While leaving the plane, the lady with the sweet voice again smiled. As I was about to ask to join me for my further journey she was already looking at the next person with the same smile. I was expecting this usually-experienced disappointment and forgot the same, as at the door there was 'My Mumbai'.

Somebody was waving his hands while stepping down, somebody else was giving a formal welcome, and somebody was holding a nameplate or a board bearing a company name. We accepted everybody's welcome as there was no one to receive us.

I ran inside the bus. I was the first on the bus and seated in a corner. As I turned back, I saw a sparrow returning from another journey or to rest. I was the last one off the bus.

Now I had to search for my bag first. It arrived happily on a conveyer as it had enjoyed the flight journey a lot. The same facility should be provided for school children carrying heavy bags on their small backs. Is it possible?

Home Sweet Home

I came out of Airport proudly with my bag on my back. Though I am a local boy, local actually & we ruled here. I was surprised after hearing the Fare told by an Auto rickshaw driver at Airport. Then I decided to go for a Bus, I caught a slowly running bus while walking & returned to the original role of a local Mumbai passenger. I asked the conductor about the bus, whether it will move towards the direction of Bhandup. After confirmation only, then I had taken a ticket. The bus stopped in expected traffic for some time & then I felled that, yes this is actual Mumbai. I left the bus in between and not at the particular stop. Just said Bhandup & without any bargaining rickshaw driver agreed because fare will base on meters after getting down. If I would take a rickshaw from the airport charges would be more. Now I was just waiting for a moment of reaching my Sweet home. After half an hour, the rickshaw stopped at the entrance of alleys. I was walking on the road proudly. Of course, all the things were as it is. But my approach was changed. The whole world was so beautiful. Base camp plays the most important role in my life.

And I reached the holiest huge palace….my home. With a new birth, new energy, new rays of hopes, new dreams, new gossips, new experiences, new steps & a totally new version of Mine, I entered.

Mom & a neighbor stopped talking & welcomed

without any word as expected. Having a bath with soap & hot water at home felt so relaxed. I praised God who was the support for us for the days in between the total Trek Journey. I listened to the reaction after telling the mishap of losing the camera. According to My Mother, the biggest thing is that - I had returned home back properly. After this reaction, I could not tell here about the tattoo on a right shoulder Accidently drawn in an accident.

A Fish Fry Dish was waiting for me to make him free. I completed his wish with my Hunger. Father called my Mother for my home arrival Confirmation. Because of my love for fish, I left the conversation with Him.

I started removing the things one after one from a bag. Those were not normal things and were part of special memories. To share the happiness with Family boxes of Pethas from Agra came out first. A blanket used only at Hostel & gave a feeling of slipping at home came afterward. A wire of toy was stuck in a blanket. Clothes took care of each body part, then the medicine, not used at all, a pant which was not used, a cap without feather, special clothes used for 7 continuous days are treated as part of the body itself; clothes can be used in the next Himalaya journey only put out of the box. Each of the items started reminding all incidents.

Some objects did not come at all. Hand gloves were lost in an accident on the bus; Snacks finished immediately after completing the trek; very very important, one of my friends, a camera; could not be found at all. Some objects came out unnecessarily. It was most needful that time but could not found that was the second battery of torch. Another pair of hand gloves kept at base camp, whose importance was neglected by me. Extra Batteries of a camera is still waiting for a new camera. After removing all the things from the bag I came out of home & reversed the bag & shake it.

Some of the items entered in my bag when it was open at the moment of the accident….so many tiny pieces of glass.

I removed a binocular which has to be returned to a friend & removed a very special memorial item from it………a bark of birch.

On the same day, I had to left from office. I was a little upset that the Ceremony for the last 16 days has ended. But as I get down, Nature sent an important gift for me & for Mumbai on 16 May 2011 at 2:30 p.m., the first day of rain.